WLTM

Also by Donal Ruane

Tales in a Rearview Mirror
I'm Irish: Get Me Out of Here!

WLTM

306.73

DONAL RUANE

Gill & Macmillan

Gill & Macmillan Ltd
Hume Avenue, Park West, Dublin 12
with associated companies throughout the world
www.gillmacmillan.ie

© Donal Ruane 2006

ISBN-13: 978 07171 3989 7
ISBN-10: 0 7171 3989 1

Typography design by Make Communication
Print origination by Carole Lynch
Printed by Nørhaven Paperback A/S, Denmark

This book is typeset in Minion 10pt on 12.5pt.

The paper used in this book is made from the wood pulp of
managed forests. For every tree felled, at least one tree is
planted, thereby renewing natural resources.

A CIP catalogue record for this book is available
from the British Library.

5 4 3 2 1

Me duelen los ojos de mirar sin verte

'Time ticks by; we grow older. Before we know it, too much time has passed and we've missed the chance to have had other people hurt us. To a younger me this sounded like luck; to an older me this sounds like a quiet tragedy.'

—DOUGLAS COUPLAND
LIFE AFTER GOD

01

Not being one to do things by halves, I made four New Year's resolutions for 2004, even though historically I have set very little store by them, principally because their self-improvement/remedial nature involves me spending time doing something I don't particularly want to do but feel I should do, leaving me with less time to do something I would like to do.[1]

Another reason I'm not big into New Year's resolutions is because so many aspects of my character warrant attention and improvement, that a month is normally gone before I've managed to whittle down this very long longlist to a more manageable and deceptively attainable shortlist,[2] with the result that I then feel

1. Which in an ideal world would be to do nothing at all; something which, ironically, quite often takes me longer to do than doing something which I don't particularly want to do but feel I should do: it takes many, many hours to fully attain that state of inner calm where I can finally relax, safe in the knowledge that I am absolutely, positively, doing nothing.

2. Unlike traditional shortlists, there is no eventual 'winner' resolution selected from mine. I think it's best to have a few options open to you so that when one resolution is abandoned for whatever reason, there are still a couple of others left to plough on with for another little while, until such time as the whole enterprise is fully and finally abandoned.

slightly cheated because I've only got eleven months left to implement the selected resolutions. And so that list inevitably falls by the wayside, where it remains until January of the following year when the unresolved resolutions come up for consideration again, by which time they are then competing with other, newer resolutions which have come to mind over the preceding year. And so, once again, a new shortlist is confirmed at the end of that January, and this new list is pinned to the pine-framed cork notice board in my head. (Buying a real pine-framed cork notice board was a New Year's resolution of mine in 2002, one which sadly went unimplemented, and which, after due consideration, didn't make the shortlist for 2003, so a metaphorical one has to suffice.) Being a creature of habit, a couple of months into the new New Year, that list will eventually slip off the pine-framed cork notice board in my head and fall by the wayside as well, resulting in yet another year passing with me making little or no progress on my much-needed rehabilitation.

After failing to find a third party on whom I could somehow lay the blame for my abject failure to successfully implement any of the previous few years' resolutions, I reluctantly conceded that it was in fact my own inactivity—my own proactively inactive inactivity—which was to blame for the non-implementation of those same resolutions. In an effort to counteract the unfortunate situation where successive New Year's resolutions had gone unimplemented, for 2004, I created two separate longlists, the first one revolving around things I *didn't* particularly want to do, and the second one revolving around things I *did* want to do.

After much whittling I finally reduced the two longlists to two shortlists. On the first shortlist were:

1. I will set greater store by New Year's resolutions (best to walk before one attempts to run, no?) and,
2. I will learn to give myself the benefit of the doubt.

And on the eminently more preferable shortlist were:

1. I will spend as much time as possible doing absolutely nothing; and,
2. I will take off for a few months (say, about four) and go deep-sea treasure hunting somewhere hot.

The above list of four resolutions was, as I'm sure you can appreciate, the result of much utterly exhaustive deliberation. So much so, that it was, predictably enough, the end of January before I had the whittling process complete and was able to finally draw up my two shortlists. Somewhat miffed at having already lost a month in terms of the standard timeframe allowed for the successful implementation of New Year's resolutions, I cleverly decided to abandon the Gregorian calendar used throughout the world and reverted instead to the ancient Chinese lunar calendar,[3] effectively meaning that as at 29 January 2004, the date my two shortlists were drawn up, it was actually only the eighth day of my new year, as the Chinese New Year began on 22 January.

My lists of resolutions were also very cleverly constructed, in that the implementation of resolution number two on the first don't-want-to shortlist and both resolutions on the second, were in fact dependent on the *prior* and successful implementation of resolution number one on the first shortlist. And so, on 29 January 2004, I stood in front of the bathroom mirror and calmly told myself that, far from being something to be abandoned at the first available opportunity, New Year's resolutions were an established,

3. The Chinese New Year begins on the second New Moon after the Winter Solstice. The Chinese calendar actually dates back long before the Gregorian calendar we all know and take for granted nowadays, which itself is a 1582 modification of the Julian calendar favoured by Julius Caesar in ancient Rome, which is fair enough, because he established it. The Chinese calendar measures time based on astronomical observations of the movement of the Sun, Moon and stars. Furthermore, according to the Chinese lunar calendar, 2004 isn't actually 2004 at all. It's 4071, the year of the Green Monkey. Best of all though, 4071 is a leap year, and the clever Chinese, what with their penchant for festivals and fireworks, add a whole month on in a leap year, and not a paltry day like we do in the West.

acknowledged and useful self-help mechanism, and that if anyone was in need of some self-help, it was myself.

There. Done. One down, three to go. Piece of cake. Rock on, 4071.

After finalising my two shortlists I decamped to southern Spain for a while in February (even though technically it was still only 12 January), ostensibly to make some serious progress on my second book, something I was finding difficult to do at home. On my return, I looked over the quantity and quality of what I had written, and, with some surprise and not a little disappointment, discovered that I had achieved pretty much the same as I would have had I remained at home and sat in the kitchen for six or seven hours every night. I was surprised because, whilst away in the not-so-sunny climes of the Costa del Sol, I had been operating on the now incontrovertibly deluded notion that my work rate had improved enormously and that I was at last acquiring something approaching discipline where serious matters such as deadlines were concerned.

More importantly though, my disappointment lay not with the quantity and quality of what I had written, but with the fact that once again, I had failed to give myself the benefit of the doubt: I had reasoned to all around me that I 'needed to get away' in order to crack on with the book, declaring that the solitude of my sister's apartment in Spain would be just the thing to facilitate me making the real and substantive progress I had been yakking on about making for the previous couple of months. And yet the simple fact of the matter was, I didn't trust myself to deliver the book to my publisher on time were I to remain in Dublin because of the numerous 'distractions' around me.[4]

Of all things to confer on oneself, you'd think that the benefit of the doubt would be one of the easier ones, but no, I couldn't even manage that. And my inability to do just that had for far too long plagued another area of my life, one of much greater concern to

4. Such distractions included daytime TV, nighttime TV, late-night TV, my expanding DVD collection, my bed and surfing the net for the books, movies and CDs I had convinced myself I could not live without.

me than my 'professional' one—my personal life. To the extent that I didn't have one. Apart from the relationship I had with myself, of course, which, though at times immensely satisfying and fulfilling, was at other times—such times increasingly appearing to be most of the time—excessively introverted and devoid of variety, given how well I have come to know myself over the years.

That was part of the problem too: I knew myself too well. To the extent that over the same years, I had formed very concrete ideas about the type of soulmate/lover/girlfriend/partner/confidante who would best suit my needs, and had all but discounted any hope of ever meeting such a specimen.

Of course, had I deigned to formulate the idea from the other end of the equation and assessed how attractive a soulmate/lover/boyfriend/partner/confidante I shaped up to be, replete as I am with many flaws, chief amongst them my reluctance to remedy them, I might have realised that instead of arrogantly concluding that there were very few women out there who would be suitable for me, I would have arrived at the decidedly more sobering conclusion that there were in fact very few women out there who would put up with an asshole of my magnitude for any length of time.

Wait, though. Was I being too hard on myself? Fair enough, I'm an asshole, but everybody else is too, some even to a greater degree and many of them with a higher frequency than me. God knows I've seen enough of them in action, and yet most of them managed to string a girl along nonetheless. The way I saw it, I simply hadn't gotten the exposure I needed over the last few years. In a city of over a million people, there had to be at least a few women out there who would find what I had going for me worth the effort involved in ascertaining exactly what it was I had going for me. So that was it: I had to get out there and find one of them. Or at least make an effort to find one of them. Blind dates. Personal ads. Chance encounters. Stalking. It was all up for grabs.

02

The day after returning from the aforementioned writing retreat in Spain, I sifted through a satisfyingly large batch of mail that had arrived in my absence. My satisfaction dissipated to a large degree when I discovered that most of the envelopes contained nothing more exciting than bills or unsolicited offers of credit which my self-employed status excluded me from accepting. Amongst the pile, however, was an envelope bearing the logo of my publisher. Fantasising about the film rights to my first book being snapped up by Working Title, I greedily tore open the envelope, only to find another envelope, bright red in colour. And inside that envelope was a Valentine's card of all things.

I should point out that this was the first truly unsolicited Valentine's card I had ever received. I accept that the phrase 'un-solicited Valentine's card' might seem tautological to those of you with a keen eye for the grammatically correct, but I mean in the sense of it having been the first such card I received when alto-gether not expecting it. Obviously, if you're going out with some-one in and around the much loathed day in question, the least you expect is one card from your significant other, if for no other reason than to balance the scales of reciprocity, allowing you to take comfort from the knowledge that they, too, had to make a last-minute dash to the newsagents and post office to fulfil the rigorous obligations of the occasion imposed by Hallmark. I attribute the fact that I have never received unsolicited Valentine's cards to the fact that my correspondence details, and those of my family, have always remained ex-directory. There is a very good reason why this is so, but nonetheless, I have no doubt that the absence of such details put paid to many potentially amorous teenage liaisons.

But now I had broken my duck, as they say. Inside the frankly quite tawdry and apparently hastily chosen card was a simple enough message: '*Just read your book—it made me laugh. I think you could make me smile.*' An initial, what appeared to be an 'I', followed, accompanied by a mobile number. I tapped the card against my chin for a minute or two, trying to think who it could be from. A couple of months previously I had broken up with an I-initialled woman, but dismissed the prospects of the card being from her, firstly because she knew my actual postal address, and secondly because it didn't strike me as the kind of thing she would have done were we still romantically involved, having shown herself to be something of an unsentimental individual where such matters were concerned, though one who would ironically take great offence at not being the recipient of a Valentine's card herself.

Satisfied that the origin of the card was a genuine mystery, I had to decide on my response. If there was to be one at all. I could, and maybe should, just take it at face value: someone out there, hopefully female, had read my book, thought it was kind of funny and seeing as how her thoughts had coincided with the drawing near of Valentine's Day, decided to send me a card. I could just leave it at that, and I, along with my fertile imagination, would be the winner. On the other hand though, if I gave myself the benefit of the doubt and allowed myself consider that the sender was an attractive, single female, currently living in Dublin but keen to relocate to southern France, interested in the arts and something of a *bon viveur*, and I replied to the number with a witty and mildly suggestive message, and things developed, then ... then who knows what might happen? Moreover, it was a perfect opportunity to get started on the hunt for a soulmate/lover/girlfriend/partner/confidante.

As is the way with the debates that constantly rage inside my head, a compromise of sorts was reached. A response would be sent—it was the right thing to do—but one of acknowledgement only: I didn't want things getting out of hand right away because when they fell apart in ruin, as they surely would for such was my destiny in these matters, then I'd be the loser and would seriously regret having given myself the benefit of the doubt. This way I was both complying with my newly made resolution and insulating myself against such a downfall. And besides, what did I know about this person at this stage? Absolutely nothing. It could have been a guy who sent the card for all I knew! Who knows? Though the vast majority of the unsolicited commendatory e-mails I had previously received were from females, through my style of writing I could unwittingly have built up an image in the gay community as something of an icon. These things happen.

So that was that: a thanks for the card and a harmless quip about how atrocious 'her' writing was because I couldn't make out the initial on the card, thereby leaving the way open for 'her' to reply with her full name, should 'she' wish to continue the communication. I could then assess the tone of the non-verbal message and take things from there. God, the stress of this was freaking me out already! I activated the own-number-sending facility on my mobile so 'she'd' have a return path should 'she' wish to respond, composed my text message, signed off with my first name (it was now early March—maybe 'she'd' forgotten about the whole thing not having received a reply before this), and pressed 'Send'.

I left it at that and got back into my usual routine, which involved little more than simultaneously booting up both my computer and my TV. An hour or so later, the familiar 'beep-beep' alert was heard from the kitchen where I had my phone charging. The message was from my anonymous admirer all right, but was not what I had envisaged. '*Who is this?*' it read. Disgusted, I threw the phone down on the table, raging I had even partially given myself the benefit of the doubt and thought for one minute that something interesting and fulfilling might come out of the whole affair. '*Who is this?*' How many Valentine's cards had she sent? I went back to my sofa and my TV and silently pondered my next move. Maybe I should leave well enough alone. I hadn't, as yet, made a complete tit of myself. If I sent another message, outlining who exactly I was, it might look a bit desperate.

But then again, when a reply hadn't been received within a few days of Valentine's Day, maybe my mystery admirer had forgotten the whole thing, put it out of 'her' head and got on with 'her' life? Or maybe my text message was too vague? Another, more comprehensive one might clear things up and refresh 'her' memory, I thought, and dispatched same, outlining my six-week absence from Dublin and hence the delay in acknowledging my receipt of the card. A few minutes later, another 'beep-beep', and bingo, the penny had dropped, the lines of communication were open, and over the next couple of hours, numerous texts were sent and received, with my admirer (now officially female), suggesting that, '*we cud meet up if u like*'. Glad to have the possibility of rejection eliminated from the proceedings in the event of *my* suggesting that we could meet up, I casually assented and suggested The Long Hall that Friday night, at 8 o'clock. Her approval duly arrived, along with some supporting information—'*Im 5'6" n blonde*'.

Paul (a good friend since my college days) called over to discuss tactics for the date. Since he got married last year, his opportunities for bounding around and behaviour of a caddish nature have obviously (and quite rightly) been seriously limited, so he heartily endorsed my decision to get out there and meet some women, electing himself my 'life coach' for the duration of the experiment.[1] After outlining 'our basic strategy' for the night ahead on my whiteboard for twenty minutes—mindlessly rubbing out the plot outline of the epic novel I had recently embarked on—I asked him to leave.

Friday rolled around and I headed into town, parking myself on a stool in The Long Hall at 7.30 to get a couple of beers into me

1. Two things you ought to know about Paul: one; he has genuine difficulty constructing a full sentence without making use of some sporting analogy or metaphor, usually soccer-related; and two, when referring to any of his close associates, he uses the royal 'we' and its associated variants constantly.

before show time. I cleverly sat one stool up from the end of the bar, leaving the very last stool out of commission for all but a lone drinker, hoping to retain it for my companion so that we could have a cosy corner to ourselves as we got to know each other. This strategic position also had the benefit of allowing me to utilise the heavily mirrored wood panelling behind the bar to check out everybody that came in. There was even a clock on the wall behind me so I could keep track of time and know when to begin paying extra attention to blonde single female arrivals, of approximately 5'6" in height.

So, 7.55 crept up on me, I was well into my second bottle of Miller, and this absolute babe arrived into the bar. I straightened up, not able to believe my luck. Okay, she was taller than 5'6", but she had got blonde hair, was on her own, and was cautiously advancing along the bar counter as if on the lookout for an unfamiliar face. This could be it, I thought. How sweet was this? Just back from Spain after a painful four weeks deluding myself into thinking I was getting loads of work done, after the worst Christmas on record, with no money, no job (unless you count being a full-time writer), and out of the blue, a very cool, independent, and very cute blonde goes out on a limb, sends me a Valentine's card, and here I am, on the cusp of something potentially great.

(Now, you may think I was getting carried away here, but I wasn't really. This chick was very cool, I could tell by looking at her. She wasn't an accountant or a legal secretary or anything like that. She had more of a graphic-designer/media/music-industry vibe about her, but not in a wannabe way, her look just reflected the circles she moved in: quirky but cool jewellery and an eclectic fashion sense that just worked, and lent her an air of self-assured independence.

That might sound like an awful lot to ascertain about someone after having just seen them sidle cautiously along a bar counter, not having actually spoken a single word to them, but trust me, this is my thing: I'm incredibly nosy, very, very observant and during my time served as a Dublin city taxi driver, I have over the years met tens and tens of thousands of different people, so I reckon I can fairly accurately gauge what kind of person somebody is just by looking at them. Might sound very judgemental, and it is a bit, I suppose, but really what I'm saying is that I'm confident I can tell straight away if someone is a tosser or not, and whether I have any interest in finding out more about them.[2])

So, my media babe was approaching. I let her go by into the back section, just to be on the safe side—there were a lot more people in there and maybe she was meeting someone there, if she was not my date. She went through the arch, had a scan around and started to make her way back. This was looking good, so I got myself together and swung around on my stool, on the verge of casually saying, 'Hi, you must be Susan',[3] when I heard her say, 'Hi babes! Oh, it's so good to see you! Look at the colour of you!' to another chick who had just come into the bar. Devastated, I completed my futile 360° revolution. Shit. Why not? Why for once didn't things pan out the way I wanted them to? She was cool. And such a sound chick as well, meeting up with her recently returned buddy at the first available opportunity to see how she had got on wherever it was she had been. I'd say we'd have had a lot in common, me and her. That would have been good. That could have gone somewhere, I was sure of it.

Now just wait and see what arrives in, won't be anything like that at all. Probably be some perfectly pleasant woman from a good family, with a secure job, who owns her own home, pays the maximum contributions allowable into her ssia, and has a new Micra on 0 per cent finance. All the things I couldn't care less about. The next single woman who walks into this bar is yours for

2. I fully concede that such a pathetic and immature *modus operandi* is not without its shortcomings, chief amongst them the very real possibility that some day, a woman whose character, disposition, aspirations and interests I hastily, and without supporting evidence, assess and consequently dismiss, could in fact be the one woman with whom I could enjoy a stable, mutually satisfying and fulfilling relationship. (Ironically though, what will save me from having to deal with such a crushing realisation is in fact, said *modus operandi*, as the woman in question will have been dismissed out of hand, and I will never know what might have been.)

3. The initial on the card was an 'S' by the way, not an 'I'—told you her writing was atrocious.

the evening, and it's your own bloody fault. Couldn't just take the card as a bit of a laugh, allow yourself a moment's flattery and leave it at that, could you? No, you just had to push it that bit further. Well here you go, sucker . . . just desserts.

Next thing, bang on 8.00, I heard a 'beep-beep' from my mobile. I grabbed it and read the message. '*Didnt c u inside. Im outside.*' Oh God, this did not bode well. What am I doing here? Thinking I was in a movie—a horror movie—I scanned the bar, pitifully looking for an emergency exit, throwing the barman a beseeching look, hoping his years of experience would lend him sympathy for my predicament and that he would spirit me away through a warren of underground passages, depositing me on the relative safety of South Great George's Street, from whence I could grab a taxi and split home to my familiar Friday-night habitat—the sofa in my front room with a tasty meal from Supper's Ready, a glass of wine and a DVD. No emergency exits presented themselves, however, the barman was impassive to my forlorn gaze; there was nothing for it but to go forth and meet my destiny.

'Hi, you must be Susan,' I said as cheerily as I could to the sole occupant of the tiny porch outside the bar door.

'Yeah, that's me,' replied the woman (whose hair was definitely not blonde—it looked more like red to me). 'I didn't recognise you, not that I should have I suppose, seeing as how I've never met you before, ha ha. So, I thought I'd come out here and text you. I didn't even know if you were here yet, but I thought if you were, that sending you a text would be the handiest thing, instead of me walking around in there looking for someone I didn't know . . .'

Stop talking. Please stop talking. Oh, God. Oh, God, I don't feel well.

'Yeah, I know what you mean . . . well, here I am. Let's go inside. Hopefully some bastard hasn't nicked my seat,' I said, by way of something to say.

'Oh right . . . yeah, okay,' she answered, somewhat cautiously I thought.

I turned and walked back towards my thankfully still-vacant stool. The one I had been trying to keep for her had indeed been commandeered by a lone drinker, mine narrowly escaping the same fate by virtue of having my leather jacket draped over it. Shit. I really needed to sit down, didn't feel well at all. Better at least offer her the stool though.

'Tosser,' I muttered in the direction of the stool usurper, 'I was trying to keep a spare stool, but there you go. Would you like to sit down?'

'No, no, I'm fine,' she said, much to my relief.

'Fair enough,' I said, lowering myself stoolward. 'What'll you have to drink?'

'Oh, let's see . . . I'll have a red wine please. Chilean.'

'Chilean?' I repeated jocularly, gesturing towards the same barman who wouldn't cooperate with my escape plan a few minutes previously.

'Bottle of Miller and a red wine please,' I said in a friendly tone. 'Chilean, if you have it,' I added casually in a lowered voice—didn't want to cause a scene in here of all places, one of the half-dozen or so remaining bars in Dublin that didn't feel the need to have fashion police guarding the door.

'Australian's the best I can do for you,' he replied helpfully.

'Near enough,' I said, relieved the matter was resolved. She probably wouldn't be able to tell the difference anyway.

'Now, there you go,' I said, turning to face my companion once more, handing her the bottle of wine and glass.

'Thank you,' she said politely, examining the label on the bottle carefully.

Jesus, she's probably a Master of Wine, knowing my luck, working as chief *sommelier* in some swanky hotel.

'No Chilean, I'm afraid. Australian'll have to do you,' I continued, anticipitating any objection she might raise, the likelihood of which was becoming a distinct possibility, if the arching of her not-blonde eyebrows was anything to go by.

'It's near enough,' I said, repeating the witty remark I'd made to the barman a minute before.

'Geography's not your strong point, I take it?' she countered.

Now, fair enough, she was genuinely trying to be funny and parry my witty comment with a barbed riposte of her own, break the ice and all that, trying to be cool and what have you, but she ended up sounding like a narky cow. Tone and inflection are critical when making comments like that, and are best left to experts in the field. Like me. She needed to practise a little, then she'd be fine. Magnanimously, I decided to let it slide.

'No, not really,' I conceded. 'I'm sure it's grand though.'

Keen to avoid a debate about the merits of South American New World wines vis-à-vis their established Antipodean counterparts, I kicked for touch and asked her what she did.

'I'm a nurse,' she answered. 'Well, it's more occupational therapy really. I'm very interested in that whole area. And I'm also doing a course in reflexology.'

'Oh, right yeah,' I volunteered, trying to sound interested, and obviously doing far too good a job of it, because she then launched into an excessively detailed account of what constituted her average day, and how demanding it was to balance the onerous duties of her job with the amount of study and reading required of her night course.

Now again, fair enough, she was trying to make conversation and all that, but as I have said before, thanks to my finely tuned observational skills and my knack for discerning a huge amount about someone from even the most seemingly innocuous remark that they might make, I know within a very short space of time whether or not I have any interest in even getting to know them further, never mind considering the notion of moving things on to a romantic level. And at 8.08pm, I knew for a fact that as far as this perfectly pleasant woman was concerned, I didn't, and that was that.

I also knew that, much as I wanted to, it would be terribly impolite of me to inform this perfectly pleasant woman of my decision at this particularly early juncture, to bid her farewell and split home. Quite apart from it not being polite, such a candid admission could, and in all likelihood would, cause a bit of a scene, and if there's one thing I try to avoid whenever possible, it's a confrontational scene. Yeah, eight minutes into it, and you want to go home? There'd definitely be a scene:

—*Sorry, did you say you wanted to go home?*
—*Yeah . . . if that's okay with you.*

—*Well, actually, no, it's not okay with me. Why do you want to go home?*

—*I just don't think it's going to work out, that's all.*

—*You don't think what's going to work out? We've only just met, for God's sake.*

—*I know, I know . . . and I'm sure you're really nice and everything, and I'm sure you'll find someone eventually, it's just . . . it's just that I don't think you're my type really. And . . . and I'd kinda like to go home, that's all . . .*

—*I'm not your type? You arrogant shit! What makes you think you're* my *type? How do you know I'm not standing here cringing at the sight of you, regretting sending you that bloody card, and wishing I was at home? Well?*

—*That's a fair point actually . . . I said it first though, and anyway . . .*

—*I said it first though? What are you? Six? Jesus, you really are an asshole. I don't know why . . .*

—*Relax, relax. Put the bottle down. Nice and easy. Look, all I'm saying is this: I know I'm an asshole. And maybe I think you're a bit of an asshole too, nothing major maybe, I don't know you that well—don't know you at all really, if I'm honest about it. It's just I have this theory that I know within a couple of minutes whether or not I ever want to talk to someone again. Or see them again, you know? Especially with chicks . . . that's just the way it is. And I'm not getting that vibe with you, that's all there is to it. So I just thought if I went home now, it'd save me the hassle of going through the whole ritual of feigned interest and all that kind of thing. Plus, if I just split now, I can avoid that painful bit at the end of the night when, using a garbled mixture of vague and non-committal phrases, I try and communicate to you that I have no desire to see you again . . .*

Think about it. Let's just say we go through the motions for the evening, have a drink, get a bite to eat, whatever, yeah? And given my dislike of confrontation, I'm all pleasant and polite and attentive and stuff? And I can do that, I can, done it loads of times. And let's say, let's just say that at the end of the night, for whatever reason, you're mad into me and want to see me again, okay?

Because you'd built up this image of me as someone who's nice, and polite, and attentive, a good listener and all that, yeah? Well, you'd only be fooling yourself. Don't you see? 'Cos I'm not like that, I'm an asshole . . . And that's why I'd like to go home now, and avoid all that crap . . . For you and for me. Me mostly like, but for you as well . . .

No, better just plough on with it. Put up a good front and all that. Nobody forced you to be here, so just make the best of it, try and have a pleasant evening and then get away as cleanly as possible.

As these confrontational scenes were playing out in my head, and I arrived at the decision to plough on and make the best of it, I started coming over all faint and dizzy. I put it down to my disappointment at my blind date not being the cool media babe who'd arrived in at 7.55, and who was now sitting with her recently returned friend (who was also kind of cute), at the other end of the bar. She was the one I wanted to be spending my Friday night with, getting to know her and having a laugh. What a cool chick. Great ass too. Sod it, I started thinking to myself: And now I'm all hot and bothered, really hot and bothered. So much so that if I don't get to the toilet real soon and splash some cold water on my face and freshen up a bit, I'm going to faint. When did I last faint? I don't think I've ever fainted actually. No, I haven't. Imagine that—I've never fainted, and now here I am, ten minutes into my first blind date and I'm on the verge of fainting. How un-cool is that? Should have eaten something before I came out. But I thought she'd be cool, like my media babe down there, and that we'd be cruising over to Odessa or somewhere for a bite to eat. But no . . . Jesus, would she ever hurry up telling me about her bloody job and her bloody course so I can go to the loo? Could I just get up and go maybe? 'Sorry to cut across you, but I really have to go to the toilet.' God no, she's a nurse; she'll probably think I have some kind of bladder problem. Just let her finish up this and then I'll calmly excuse myself, splash some water on my face, assess the situation, and come up with a plan. Yeah, that's what I'll do after I've done the water thing, I'll come up with a plan for the rest of the evening, however long that may be, and I'll . . .

What seemed like an hour later, but was in fact probably only ten seconds . . .

'Are you okay? Can you hear me? Donal?'

Too late. I'd fainted. Right there at the bar in The Long Hall. At ten past eight on a Friday night. Slid off my stool and slumped to the ground, whacking my head off the brass railing as I went down. What a tit.

'Donal? Are you all right? Do you want to get some air?' Susan asked me in her nursey tone, clearly and loudly.

A little too loudly for my liking to be honest with you, in that it drew considerably more attention to my position on the floor than I felt was absolutely necessary, with the result that those who hadn't copped on to the drama as it actually unfolded now had to crane their heads over the numerous voyeurs who had abandoned their pints immediately to stand directly over me so they'd have the best view in case it was an aneurism and I died and they'd be able to tell their friends that they were there when your man died in The Long Hall. 'Yeah, I was sitting there with Mark, when . . . You know Mark. You do—he's in Woodbrook, plays off seven, very handy—yeah, that's the one. Anyway, myself and Mark are in The Long Hall, having a pint when your man just keeled over, fell off the stool, whacked his head off the railing, onto the floor and that was it. Dead. Stone dead. Swear to God. You can ask Mark. Ruane, his name was. Wrote that book about being a taxi driver, do you remember? Yeah, him. Bit of an asshole by all accounts. Anyway. He's dead now.'

That sort of thing. So there I was, slumped on the carpet, trying to summon whatever will to live remained in my near-lifeless body so I could get up off the floor, compose myself and make as digni-fied an exit from the bar as recently unfolded events would allow.

'Yeah, yeah, I'm grand, I'm grand. Just a little hot that's all,' I eventually replied, hoisting myself upwards.

'Do you get seizures, buddy?' this American guy earnestly enquired.

Seizures? Who the hell are you?

'No I don't,' I answered curtly, not entirely sure what a seizure was, but keen to avoid having to add it to the already overly long list of ailments and afflictions I had by now established that I did suffer from. Turning my back on the Yank and his bony girlfriend, I smiled weakly at my blind date and shrugged my shoulders.

'Seriously, I'm fine. Just a bit weak, that's all. I thought we might be getting a bite to eat so I didn't have any dinner, you know? Think I'll just go to the toilet for a minute, freshen up, okay?'

'Of course, yeah, of course. You do that,' Susan said calmly. 'And then we'll go, get you some fresh air, yeah?'

'Yeah, cool,' I replied as I made my way towards the toilets, conscious of the fact that by failing to have an aneurism and die I had disappointed quite a few of the people I was now passing, who had had to revert to the banalities of their own lives for topics of conversation.

Cold water on the face taken of, I checked myself out in the mirror. My own reflection is not normally a sight that fills me with great joy, but on this particular occasion, what with my bleary eyes and near-deathly pallor, it was pretty scary. Pining for my sofa and blissful solitude, I shook my head wearily and went back out to face the music.

'Right, that's better. Let's get out of here,' I said as cheerily as I could to Susan, who had finished her wine and was standing attentively by my stool, my jacket in her hand.

'Yeah, let's get you some fresh air and something to eat,' she agreed, holding open my jacket for me to reverse into like I was 87 years of age.

'I just fainted. I'm not infirm,' I said somewhat testily, declining to put on my jacket, casually slinging it over my shoulder as I gestured for her to make her way towards the door.

Outside on George's Street, Friday-night Dublin was moving into top gear and I realised that the chances of waltzing into a restaurant unreserved and getting a table were few and far between. The last thing I needed at this stage was to spend another forty minutes or so standing in a restaurant watching other people eat as I slavered in anticipation of getting some food into me. For a minute I thought I could use this as an out to split home, but dismissed it as soon as Susan suggested we take a rain-check and do it all over again another night the following week.

No way. However painful this whole experience was going to be, there sure as hell wasn't going to be a repeat performance.

'Not at all, I'm grand, we'll find somewhere and grab a quick bite to eat,' I said jauntily, starting across the road.

'Okay then, what do you fancy eating?'

'Oh, I don't mind, I'm not that fussy,' I lied.[4]

'How about an Indian? The Eastern Tandoori's just around the corner,' Susan ventured helpfully.

An Indian of all bloody things. I hate Indian food. I've never tried much Indian food; I just know I hate it. All that artificial colouring and excessive heat. What's the point? And yoghurts. What place do yoghurts have in an evening meal?

'Grand, yeah, sounds good,' I replied, only too happy to move things along so as I could get home and put all this behind me.

The Eastern Tandoori on South William Street was relatively quiet, thank God, and we were seated straight away. On reflection I thought this probably wasn't such a bad choice after all—ethnic restaurants are renowned for their speedy and efficient service, lashing out platters of average food to largely large and unfussy customers—so with any luck we'd be out of here in an hour or so.

After scanning the 600-item-long menu, I plumped for the most innocuous-sounding option I could find, a mild chicken curry. She went for some weird thing I can't remember the name of. Turned out she was driving that night, which, no doubt coupled with the absence of a suitable Chilean number on the wine list, meant she was happy enough to drink water. I opted for a half bottle of wine to help me through the serious feigned-interest phase we were now entering and the waiter hotfooted it off

4. I am actually incredibly fussy about what I eat, and dismiss all manner of potentially delicious foods solely on the basis of a series of highly irrational criteria. I won't eat coleslaw because it looks horrible. I won't eat a huge variety of cheeses because I can't willingly allow mould to pass through my digestive system. I won't eat rabbits because they're cute little animals. I won't eat mussels because of the excessive complexity involved in their consumption. I won't eat spicy foods because they're too spicy. I won't eat liver because it was force fed to me as a child, something I resented greatly. Ditto for parsnips and turnips. I won't eat . . . You get the idea.

towards the kitchen, from whence he returned not a minute later with wine, water, a basket of crackery things and assurances that our food would arrive shortly thereafter. Good guy, this fella—definitely on my side. Not like that bastard barman in The Long Hall. I got stuck into the wine and snapped a little piece off one of the crackery things to have a bite and see if I could eat it. Quite tasty it was too actually—turned out to be a poppadum.

As the conversation progressed from one mundane topic to the next, I had decided that my strategy for the evening would be to politely disagree with everything Susan said, in an effort to convey to her how little we had in common and how futile it would be for us to even consider the notion of our acquaintance continuing beyond this night. Unfortunately, this strategy backfired on me to some degree, in that she found my unorthodox views on most things quite hilarious, and all too often concluded her contributions with a, 'You're gas' kind of comment, which in my limited experience, can pretty much be interpreted by men as actually meaning something along the lines of 'I'll sort that out'.

By way of example:

'So, how about kids?'

'Are you mad? I can't stand kids. You have a kid and you basically deny yourself a life for twenty years. What's the point in that? However selfish it may sound, I intend to live my life solely for myself. If I ever find somebody who's cool with that mindset and is that way inclined themselves, then that's sweet. But we'd have to be singing from the same page as far as the kids thing goes.'

'Oh, come on. Kids are amazing. What can be more rewarding than bringing a life into this world, nurturing it through childhood, watching it develop as an independent person and make its own way in the world?'

'Give me a break, where'd you get that from? That's a myth. It's nothing but hard work. You don't get a day off until they're eighteen. It's all give and no get. I just don't think it's the most productive use of my time, that's all.'

'You're gas, do you know that?'

Or:

'I've never cooked a meal in my life. And I hope I never have to. It's such a complete waste of time . . .'

'But cooking's great! I find it very relaxing preparing a meal for friends, it's very satisfying seeing people really enjoy a meal you've prepared.'

'No, no. The grief of it. Shopping in speciality stores for fennel and balsamic vinegar and all sorts of wanky ingredients that most people's limited palette can't discern anyway after a few smokes and a bottle of wine? It's bullshit. And then destroying your kitchen with pots and pans all over the place, and timing everything to perfection, and then people are late arriving and it throws your whole schedule into complete and utter chaos and you end up having a shit night yourself, and then they all sod off home and you've a load of washing up to do. Where's the satisfaction in that?'

'So are you saying you wouldn't go to somebody's house for dinner if you were invited?'

'You kidding? I'd be the first one there.'

'And what about clearing up afterwards? Would you lend a hand?'

'Depends on who's there. If I reckon there'll be some juicy scandal or serious bitching going on, I'll hang around the perimeter; put away some plates and what have you. Otherwise, I'll pop outside for a smoke and leave them to it.'

'Very good of you. Not. You're gas.'

That kind of thing.

But as I said, it backfired on me. To the extent that, as we finally left the restaurant (after I picked up the €55 tab, I might add), what I thought was a mugger trying to accost me turned out in fact to be Susan forcibly linking her arm through mine, the way couples with clearly established relationship boundaries do. I said nothing at first, before deciding that now would be as good a time as any to politely bring the evening to a close.

'What say we grab a quick coffee, yeah?' she said chirpily, beating me to it.

Shit. Will this night never end?

'I don't think there's anywhere open around here,' I answered in my best mock-rueful tone, deliberately standing with my back to a late-night coffee house across the street, the fascia of which was festooned with not one but two garish neon signs blinking suggestively in the night.

'Duh, behind you,' Susan laughed, before taking what I felt was a gross liberty on the physical side of things, and turning me 180° so I was now facing the coffee house. Armlink resumed, she led me across the street, in the door and requested a table for two.

'Nothing for me thanks, I don't drink coffee,' I said to the wait-ress bluntly, trying to put a damper on what I sincerely hoped was the last phase of the evening.

'Oh really?' she replied. 'No problem, we have juices, sodas, desserts as well. You sure you wouldn't like something?' she ventured, her annoyingly chipper American twang at full pitch. Bloody yanks and their superior service economy ways!

'I'll have a Diet Coke so, thanks,' I capitulated.

Not content with a coffee, Susan ordered a dessert as well. She'd better pick up the check for this, I was thinking—if there's one thing I can't stand it's chicks who go out for the night with only their taxi fare home in their purse. More inane chit chat ensued, with my barbed comments on any given topic invariably met with no more than an endearing smile or little chuckle.

God, was this woman possessed of anything approaching perception? How could she be comfortable sitting there? Did she seriously think that we had made a 'connection' on any level? I wasn't being rude, but I had definitely moved on from the feigned-interest thing, through barely disguised indifference, and was now approaching something approaching outright petulance.

Yank returned with our beverages and Susan's dessert, depositing them on the small table with no little aplomb and an unnecessarily broad smile, which seemed to suggest to me that she was of the opinion we made a really cute couple. Horrified, I shifted my chair a little, keen to dispel any such notions from Susan's already obviously overly active mind, and counselled myself to answer any further questions cautiously, lest she pick up on something I did not her intend her to pick up on.

'So, what do you get up to most weekends?' she enquired, instantly arousing my suspicions.

'Oh, I don't really do the weekend thing,' I answered. 'With the taxiing you kinda have to work Friday and Saturday nights if you're gonna make anything at all, you know? It's very anti-social really.'[5]

'Doesn't seem to leave you with a whole lot of time for going out then, does it?'

'No, not really. There's nobody around on a Tuesday or Wednesday when it suits me to go out.'

'You're going to have to do something about that if you want to find yourself a girlfriend!' Susan declared excitedly, perhaps trying to suggest that I must be blind, deaf and dumb not to recognise that the answer to my singleton status lay before my very eyes.

'Oh, I dunno, I kinda like keeping irregular hours, I'd hate to be trapped in that whole nine-to-five thing, it's not my scene really. And anyway, I'm not that pushed about meeting anybody right now, I'm quite happy with things the way they are,' I said emphatically.

There. Couldn't have made my position on the matter any clearer.

'You all set?' I asked, gesturing at her only-half-empty coffee cup.

'Sorry? Oh . . . yeah, yeah, sure, whenever you're ready,' she replied cooperatively.

'Right so. Just gonna go to the loo. Back in a minute,' I said. I didn't need to go at all, but a certain uneasiness had developed with my firm stance on the relationship thing and I reckoned a minute or two on her own would give Susan the chance to absorb

5. Such a regime was indeed quite anti-social. Or, more accurately, *had* been quite anti-social—what I omitted to tell Susan was that I had in fact stopped taxiing the previous month and was now completely free to entertain all manner of diversionary social activities. Just not with her.

the information and conclude that things between us were not going to progress beyond tonight.

Upon my return, I was pleased to find Susan standing patiently by the door. Forcing a smile, I held open the door and ushered her outside.

'So listen,' I said quite firmly, 'I had a great night, it was nice meeting you, and I hope all goes well with your course and new apartment and everything . . .'

'Yeah, I really enjoyed myself,' she interrupted with. 'Come on, I'll give you a lift home.'

'Christ on a cross! Would you ever leave me alone! This is it. We ain't never gonna see each other again. Can you not see that? You don't rock my world. And I don't rock yours. We are two totally different people. What is the point? I'll get a taxi.'

Ah no, I didn't say that. Not out loud anyway.

'Not at all, it's out of your way. I'll grab a taxi,' I said politely, buttoning up my jacket in advance of my longed-for departure.

'No, it's the least I can do after you paying for dinner. Come on, car's just around the corner,' she countered.

A cheque for €25 would have more than sufficed by way of reciprocation I thought to myself as I forlornly followed her towards her car. Once inside and on the move, so spent of smalltalk was I, that I immediately feigned great fatigue and remained silent, save for the issuance of directions to my house, which was thankfully only a couple of miles away. Susan jabbered on relentlessly, apparently choosing to interpret my silence as mute acquiescence to her babbling, in the process quite possibly, and most dangerously, convincing herself that we had much in common.

'Anywhere at all here is fine, thanks, I'm only around the corner,' I said as we approached the village, desperately wanting out of the car as soon as possible before I said something I might later not regret.

'Are you sure, I thought you said you were further up?' she queried.

I was. Quite a bit further up the road actually, but I was looking forward to the opportunity the walk would afford me to calm down after my bruising, near-four-hour ordeal.

'No, I'm just around the corner. You know where you are now to get home, don't you?' I asked attentively as I took off my seat-belt and made for the door.

'I do yeah, thanks,' she said as she pulled in to the kerb, before releasing her own seatbelt and shifting around to face me.

What's this about? Don't tell me she's expecting a bit of action? No way.

'Well, listen, thanks again for the lift, and all the best with every-thing, it was nice to meet . . .' I said cheerily as I opened the door.

Oh, shit. Here she comes. Eyes closed. Lips puckered. What to do? Oh, shit.

I shifted around in my seat quickly so that I was facing her cheek on as opposed to lips on, and planted the lightest kiss pos-sible. I reversed out of the car into an upright position, stuck my head in the door and said a quick, 'All the best' before closing it firmly and starting across the road, not looking back until I had safely reached the other side, from where I gave her a cheery wave.

The car pulled away, and I lit a cigarette. That was close.

———

'Why didn't you get stuck in there?' Paul asked in disbelief when we spoke on the phone the next day. (He had texted me the previous evening looking for a progress report.)

'Because I couldn't stand her; she was a pain in the arse. Especially after I fainted—I think she thought she had the upper hand or something.'

'I don't believe this. Could have been a great start to the season. And she was all on for a bit of back-seat education?'

'Yeah, seatbelt off, came straight at me. I couldn't get over it. She obviously hadn't been reading any of the signals I was giving her . . .'

'Signals, schmignals. You should have got stuck in there, man. It's like the League Cup—everybody says they're not interested in it, but it's still a bit of silverware in the old cabinet, you know?'

'What are you talking about?'

'Listen, I have to go. Rach is dragging me off to a bloody garden centre. Talk to you soon, yeah?'

'Fair enough. Good luck.'

03

Though I was lucky to get away with my life on that particular occasion, I decided to plough on regardless and explore other avenues to see if I couldn't get me a little lovin'. Before ploughing on though, I thought it best to take a day or so to draw up a few governing rules for the exercise. Without rules all would descend into chaos—that much was for sure. (Given my track record with members of the opposite sex all could very well descend into chaos anyway, but I reasoned I'd feel better about that happening if I had drawn up a set of rules and made at least a token effort to abide by them.)

The first rule I decided to adopt was the exclusivity rule, a concept much favoured by Americans, something at odds with the fact that it makes quite a lot of sense. As I understand it, when Americans begin seeing someone new, it's generally accepted that each party is free to meet and date other new people until such a time as they agree (with either the person they began seeing first or someone they met subsequently), that there is a 'connection' between them, something that is worth building on, and that from that point onwards, they will see only each other—exclusively. This saves them the hassle of spending a few weeks or months going out with somebody only to realise that they're not suited at all, and then they have to start trawling the personal ads and what have you afresh, and quite reasonably bemoan the few weeks or months they wasted with the unsuitable candidate.

Made perfect sense to me—I hadn't got the time, or the inclination, to confine myself to one candidate alone and to wait for things to run their course. There was, of course, the very real possibility that many, if not all, of the candidates I ended up dating would find me, from the off, to be a most unsuitable candidate, thereby rendering the convenience of the exclusivity rule utterly meaningless. Be that as it may, my adoption of the exclusivity rule goes back to the benefit-of-the-doubt thing: I am, in a radical break from tradition, giving myself the benefit of the doubt that one or more of the females I accompany on a first date will find me sufficiently attractive to make the prospect of a follow-up date something that doesn't make them come over all nauseous.

The second rule concerns itself with the whole notion of aesthetics, something I make no apologies for whatsoever. Whilst I know that beauty is only skin deep, I also know pure ugly goes all the way to the bone. I like things that are possessed of a certain beauty, in terms of both form and function. It's a design aesthetic, simple as that. In all aspects of my life, I will always choose the most beautiful option open to me. I will gladly pay more for the most beautiful object in question, and if that is something that is beyond my reach at a given point in time, I will happily postpone the purchase of said item until such time as I can afford it.[1] I am not, I hasten to add, referring to women as objects here—I'm just

1. By way of example, let me quickly outline to you the twofold reason behind my not having worn a wristwatch in the last 13 years. The first fold goes back to my twenty-first birthday, when I was presented with a perfectly respectable looking Rotary wristwatch. I wore the watch on my left wrist quite happily until the battery ran out a little over a year later. A watch with an expired battery is of little use, I'm sure you'll agree, so I took it off and put it somewhere safe. For safekeeping. Where it remains safe to this day, principally because I can't remember where I put the bloody thing.

So that's fold number one—I have a watch, I just can't find it. Fold number two is more telling, though. Some time after the expiration of the battery and the watch's subsequent deposit in a now un-recollectable place for safekeeping, I came across the exquisite range

making the point that, heretofore, my considered opinion on the notion of aesthetics has largely been confined to the acquisition of inanimate objects, such as art, furniture, cars etc. and that I intend to carry that discerning level of taste with me as I pursue my quest.

I do not intend to go to extremes on this score however. Beauty is most definitely in the eye of the beholder, and whomsoever I may deem an attractive woman may not do it for you, but no matter: suffice to say that in my romantic past, whilst quantity has most definitely been sorely lacking, I'm pleased to report that quality has not. All the women I've dated in the past have been very easy on the eye.[2] Most certainly on my eyes, and

1. *contd* of timepieces lovingly handcrafted by the Jaeger-LeCoultre company, high in the Jura mountains in Switzerland. After perusing the company's portfolio, I declared the Reverso Duo to be my watch of choice. (The eagle-eyed amongst you may recall that a watch from the Reverso range was worn by shoe shop owner Lucien in the rather splendid French film *L'Appartement*.) Assembled by master craftsmen, the Reverso Duo is timekeeping excellence at its most excellent. As the name implies, the watch, like quite a few people known to me, has two faces. The ingenious bit though, is that both faces are powered by the same mechanism, some elements of it working in a clockwise direction, and some elements of it working in an anti-clockwise direction. Internal workings aside, the design of the watch casing and strap, and their subsequent manufacture from white gold, also merit special mention for their refined sophistication.

   Needless to say, such a watch doesn't come cheap. The membership fee to join the Jaeger-LeCoultre club at the level I desire would leave me with little change from €10,000, which in my present circumstances is, most unfortunately, a bridge too far. And so, until my fiscals ameliorate to the point where such an acquisition would not leave me wanting, I am content to wear the decidedly more humble wristwatch which I already own. If I ever find it.

2. On reflection, the use of the word 'all' here may be somewhat misleading, in that it implies the quantity in question to be of a certain magnitude. The actual number of women involved would be somewhere between four and eleven, depending on where you draw the line between mere conquest and something of a more emotionally nourishing and fulfilling nature.

from the wistful glances I have seen numerous Lotharios cast in their direction as if I did not exist, to quite a number of others', too.[3]

When I consider a particular woman's aesthetic qualities, I focus firstly and primarily on the face, and then move on to the body, before finally, after much subtle interrogation, deciding whether or not there appears to be an alert mind and soulful soul present to complement these aesthetic features should they be to my liking. Perfectly appropriate behaviour I think. For the record, I have in the past, on occasion, managed to sublimate my liking for a pretty package, so enthralled have I been by what lay inside.[4]

3. On a purely aesthetic level, quite how I managed to be associated with such attractive women is something that is beyond me, given that I have always believed that in life, you only get as good as you give, and on this purely aesthetic level, I currently don't give a whole lot. Put another way, I also give too much, in that I presently weigh in at 175 lbs, which combined with my height of 5' 10" gives me a BMI of 25.1. Which while comfortably below the obesity threshold of 30, means I could do with shedding a few pounds. But hey, so could most chicks out there, so I'm not too worried about it yet.

4. The woman in question was so captivating that I happily overlooked her disproportionate waistline, *derrière* and thighs. It wasn't until our second date that I had a chance to furtively ascertain the expanse of the regions in question, allowing my eyes to do some comprehensive reconnaissance via a decorative mirror conveniently hung at angle of approximately 22° on the north wall of the restaurant in question, as my companion made her way towards the ladies bathroom. (Our first date had involved going to the cinema on a busy Saturday night, thus eliminating the chance of any exploratory moves on my part, should I have felt the desire to do so, which I had, obviously, but didn't follow through on, for two very good reasons. The first was that, as I said, it was a busy Saturday night and such promiscuous activity would not have gone unnoticed or uncensured by the other patrons of the Screen cinema. And quite rightly too, for apart from being my favourite place in Dublin, the Screen cinema, or any other cinema for that matter, is not the place for such carry on—people pay good money to watch a film in peace and quiet without interruption of any sort. The second reason I didn't make a move was simply good old-fashioned chivalry.) Anyway, so

They're the two major ones. Other less stringent rules, guide-lines I suppose you could call them, would be adopted in relation to various other areas of concern. Things like geography, for instance. I don't know if I've told you already or not, but, much as it dismays me, I currently find myself residing in Dublin. Which is in Ireland, for those of you who don't know. Anyhoo, for a myriad of reasons—some of which I may have cause to touch on in greater detail as we proceed—I would sooner travel to New York or Nantes to go on a date, blind or otherwise, than I would go to Dublin city centre.

That's not just because I find the architecture of my native city uninspiring, or the variety of cultural distractions available sadly lacking. No, quite apart from those very real faults—and it gives me no great pleasure to say this—it's the single people of a similar age to me living in Dublin that I find completely disappointing, particularly the females, given my heretofore unwavering hetero-sexuality.

Don't get me wrong now—Irish women are possessed of cer-tain qualities you won't find in a lot of women of any other nationality: an earthiness and warmth that is genuinely very endearing. It's just that I find most of them of them very . . . con-tained. And self-contained. And not in a good way. Ultimately contained in a vacuum of insularity and tradition, despite their outward protestations to the contrary; and utterly self-contained in an arrogant complacency no doubt derived from our recent economic 'good fortune'. Harsh words maybe, but that's the way it appears from where I'm standing. On the other hand, European women, so far as I can see and have experienced, are possessed of many alluring qualities that you'll not find in too many Irish women, notably a distinctly liberal and progressive outlook on life, something I rate very highly. Berry brown skin does a lot for

4. *contd* impressed was I with myself for not being the slightest bit put out by these somewhat disappointing and hitherto semi-vital statis-tics, that it was all I could do to restrain myself from shouting after her as she strode elegantly across the restaurant, 'God, your arse is massive and you've a bit of a belly on you, but I'm still kinda mad about you! Isn't it great?'

me too, if I'm being honest about it. Maybe I'll be proved wrong in relation to everything I've just said, who knows? I'm just throwing it out there.

Next up is the kids thing. As I alluded to before, I can't stand kids. That's all there is to it. Give me an articulate young person who can communicate with his or her elders and has interests and opinions, and that's fine. But kids themselves are a problem for me. How are you supposed to know what they want when all they do is yell, scream and cry? And I can't understand how they're so selfish, believing that since their birth your sole function in life is to attend to their every whim and desire. I also have a problem with the financial demands they put on your wallet.[5] And it freaks me out the way they're so destructive and utterly mindless of the value things may have. Without giving it a first, never mind a second thought, children will, within a matter of minutes, quite happily displace every single item within an entire household, flinging photo frames onto tastefully tiled floors, hurling footwear at patio doors, upending boxes of toys onto the floor and immediately losing interest in their contents. I don't like their callous wilfulness, the way they test a parent's self-restraint, screaming to be treated like an adult and have their sugary beverage served to them in an open container before proceeding to deliberately pour it on the carpet, an icy glint in their eyes like Damien in *The Omen*. And I can't abide the way they simply refuse to do what they're told. Lack of discipline in a child is surely one of the most repellent characteristics there is, and so embarrassing when one is in polite company. It has been my experience that, when informed that a treat of some description will be forthcoming only *after* they have eaten their dinner, the standard response amongst children aged between one and fifteen seems to be the execution of an apoplectic fit and the hurling of sharp household paraphernalia, such intolerable actions quite often being followed up with a clandestine telephone call to Childline to complain tearfully about their parent's

5. A friend recently informed me that a packet of Pampers disposable nappies costs somewhere in the region of €15. And all they do is shit in them!

complete lack of concern for their welfare.[6]

And so, kids are an absolute no-no. It is quite possible that as I sally forth on my dating odyssey I may come upon a wonderful woman who ticks all the right boxes in terms of looks, personality, disposition, passions etc. who also happens to be a devoted mother of one or possibly more quite charming children. Regardless of how fantastic she is, she will be eliminated from the process, as I have no desire to be involved in the rearing of a child, especially somebody else's.

6. In the interests of accuracy, it must be recorded here that I myself was the devil child described above, and it is quite probably the now-mature recollection of some of my childhood antics that has reinforced my determination never to have any children of my own. Two examples of such intolerable behaviour should suffice:

Apparently, legend has it that on arrival in the local supermarket in the neighbourhood where I grew up, I would make straight for the pick 'n' mix sweets tantalisingly displayed in large clear perspex bowls mounted atop a stand considerately constructed so as to be just within my grasp. When brutally informed by my mother that the sweets were in fact, *not* there for my personal consumption, I would stand in the middle of the aisle with my legs splayed, motionless and open mouthed with shock, so dispossessed of my senses that I would be utterly silent for a full minute before falling to the floor and emitting a series of banshee-like wails of injustice. Clever woman that she is, my mother would take this opportunity to whip around the store, grab her few provisions, and then use my disconcerting antics as an excuse to skip the queue at the express checkout, before grabbing me with considerable force and exiting the store in an understandably flustered and mortified fashion. (The very real possibility of my being spirited away by some poor, infertile woman so desperate to have a child that she would put up my level of carry-on never seemed to perturb my mother in the slightest.)

Secondly, for many years, my family used to holiday in the then-picturesque area of Owenahincha in County Cork. We would depart southwards for the same two weeks every year, and our arrival in the seaside town coincided with the start of some local festivities. The lampposts would be garlanded with a colourful array of bunting, flags and fairy lights, and again, legend has it that I would be both utterly inconsolable and considerably miffed were I not constantly reassured that the sole purpose of the decorations was to mark my arrival in the locality.

Essentially, all I'm saying is that I'm way too selfish to have children of my own. If I had an adorable four-year-old boy and a pretty three-year-old girl, could I wake up in the morning and say, 'Think I'll take off for a couple of weeks—climb Kilimanjaro and then go on safari in Amboseli'? No, I couldn't. Well, maybe I could, at a push, but I know I wouldn't enjoy pushing a McLaren Techno XT buggy up the mountain and listening to all that 'Are we there yet?' moaning. And that's exactly the kind of thing I want to be able to do. Other people's kids are fine really, in small doses obviously, and as long as I'm not ultimately responsible for them. Kids are great, I just couldn't eat a whole one.

While I'm at it, also worthy of mention here is the issue of age. It would be generally agreed, I am sure, that there are few things more enjoyable in this life than shagging somebody many years one's junior. (Once both parties are of consenting age and spirit, I hasten to add.) And yes, I have known the wonders of such pleasures: the lithe limbs, the succulent skin, the willing mind . . . And the eyes. Yes, those young eyes: Deep with an intoxicating mixture of innocence, abandonment and joy. Conversely, many single women of older age have, to my mind, eyes that are not deep, but shallow: shallow with an enthusiasm-sapping mixture of brittleness, betrayal and lack of expectation.

Such observations relate to matters of a purely carnal nature, obviously. When it comes to a capacity for intellectual rigour and stimulation of the soul however, young women, young people in general, show themselves to be sadly lacking, so consumed are they with the peripheral ephemera of their transient lives. Older women, on the other hand, in the main, and if by virtue of nothing more than their actual chronological age, do at least have the ability to converse and engage on certain levels that their younger counterparts simply do not.

And therein lies the quandary: if they're too young they might have very little to say for themselves in relation to the world around them, howsoever pleasing their decidedly more gymnastic disposition in relation to matters of the mattress is. Too old, and the potentially genuine delights of interacting with someone with an informed and well rounded view of the world and how they see themselves in it is considerably offset by the weary cynicism such life experience has brought with it, particularly with regard to carnal pleasure and the frequency with which it should take place. A tough nut to crack, and no mistake.

04

In order to get a helicopter view of what was what in the online dating arena I did a quick search on Google and checked out a few singles sites. Some of them were so pathetic they nearly had me abandon the whole exercise there and then. Thousands of saddo geeks looking for like-minded Vulcans to mate with. Or worse, sites that professed to have 'cracked' the secret of hooking up with beautiful women. One of them, seductionscience.com, put together by a clearly unstable and wildly delusional guy called Derek Vitalio, cracked me up altogether. He promised to reveal his seduction secrets to men around the world for the paltry sum of $89.95, and his pitch sounded like Tom Cruise's Frank TJ Mackey character in *Magnolia* evangelising at full tilt.[1] Get this:

> *I discovered the secrets of speed dating women during my days as a psychology student in college. At the time, I was an inexperienced, uptight guy who had trouble even getting women to notice me at all. I could hardly even get a date, and when I did I always ended up the night alone after spending a lot of money.*

1. The woeful grammar, poor spelling and emphatic bold type are all Derek's own work, I must add.

How I Ended My Years of Sexual Frustration

Over time I became so desperate and lonely that I found myself fantasying at the lingerie section in the J.C. Penney catalog! All kidding aside, I did wind up trying one of those online 'match-maker' services. In six months I got a grand total of ONE response. The woman looked OK in the photo, but when I met her, her breasts sagged halfway to her waist and her butt rolled when she walked. I didn't want to go home to my hand once again so I blocked out all of the voices in my head that were telling me to stop.

I took her to a cheap, sleazy motel for a one night stand, imme-diately dimmed the lights, and watched in horror as she took off her clothes and literally attacked me! I had reached the ultimate low point of my sex life. After driving home from this traumatic experience, I said to myself 'never again'. I knew I deserved to have quality women in my life, but for some reason it just wasn't happening.

For months I began to search for an answer. My salvation came in a form that I did not expect. As a psychology student, I was very interested in how the mind works. So in looking for work experience, I found an ad by a Neuro-Linguistic Programmer and looking for an intern to help her in her practice. She liked me so she hired me on the spot.

*She, being both a beautiful woman and very knowledgeable in the inner workings of the female mind, over the next year taught me how to develop **an incredible, laid back and confident atti-tude** that I had never had before. She showed me how to give off and project **a charismatic and sexual aura** that somehow touched everyone I met.*

***Imagine** my surprise when, for the very first time, I got incred-ible rapport with a green-eyed, Latin woman who worked out at my gym. Her tight behind formed a perfect heart-shape when she walked and her skin glowed a golden cinnamon brown. At first I thought, there's no way this girl would even notice me, let alone make a fast seduction—she's way out of my league. But as we talked, I was shocked at how well she responded to me. Later that night, as she kept repeating 'I can't believe I'm doing this'. I discovered she loved giving head and I had the most incredibly*

38

*satisfying night of my life. Later she told me that she liked me so much because I gave off this sexy, masculine energy that she had never felt with **any** man before. I found that night that no feeling—no feeling in the world—is as incredible as waking up next to a beautiful woman in the morning . . . a beautiful woman eager to please you in every way. It's an incredible feeling that few men will ever experience in their lifetimes and that **no amount of money can ever buy you.***

A few weeks later, I met a nice girl from France at a bar who was in the U.S. on vacation and we eventually ended the night at my apartment slowly rubbing each other down with scented oils and soap. There's nothing else like watching a nice girl dressed in bubbles—go down on you. As I began to be with more women, I even started having trouble keeping track of them. I began to think of all of the great guys out there like you and me, who really deserved better in life and could transform our lives with this obscure, but extremely powerful knowledge.

*So over the next few years I developed a simple, workable system based on scientific testing that **anyone** can learn to transform themselves into a speed dating master in literally no time: The Seduction Science System.*

Isn't that hysterical? The text is broken up with photos of incredibly gorgeous women, many of whom are, no doubt, Derek's own conquests. Check it out for yourself. If it's still live that is—with any luck the guy will have been busted by the trading standards authorities.

I suppose it's a given that a site, particularly one run by Americans, claiming to have the power to assist men in decoding the secrets behind the female psyche would be pathetic in both form and content, but some of those dedicated to helping the fairer sex attract Mr Right are equally pathetic. Whilst checking out the speed dating thing in Ireland, I came across SpeedDater.ie, which had a section on it written by one Lisa Daily, author of '*Stop Getting Dumped!: All you need to know to make men fall madly in love with you and marry 'The One' in three years or less.*' (Great title, isn't it? Such economy. So snappy.) As I read Lisa's contributions to the site, it became clear that she actually wrote very little of her own stuff, preferring to call on the help of 'experts' in related fields to bolster her own credibility as an authority on matters of the heart. In a lengthy piece entitled *'Five Secrets to Attracting the Opposite Sex'*, with a cutesy sub-heading *'Like Ants to Strawberry Jam'*, Lisa revealed the secret of how to 'quintuple your odds of winning in the dating game'.

The first pearl of wisdom was to position yourself as the centre of attention, because according to a Dr Albert Mehrabian, apparently an 'internationally-known expert in the field of spatial psychology', 'where you are in a room (and what you're doing) has a lot to do with your ability to attract the opposite sex. Where should you be for the highest impact and the greatest number of interested cuties? Smack-dab in the center of the room, standing up and moving around a bit.' (The folks behind *SpeedDater.ie* are obviously so thrilled to have secured the services of somebody as authoritative as Lisa Daily, author of the aforementioned snappily titled tome, '*Stop Getting Dumped!: All you need to know to make men fall madly in love with you and marry 'The One' in three years or less*', that they didn't feel it necessary to anglicise her text.)

Complete and utter rubbish as far as I'm concerned. Any woman who consciously tries to be the centre of attention is totally insecure, needy and very high maintenance, and would consequently not get a minute's attention from me. On the rare occasions when I do go out socially, I am always more drawn to women who move around the perimeter of the action and look as though as they would rather be somewhere else. Probably because I would too, and reckon we might have a laugh at everyone else's expense, cynically belittling the enforced jollity that surrounds us like an airborne virus.

The second step involved in reducing men to mere ants who will slaver over your strawberry-jam-like form was the '*color* lure'. (Color? It just looks wrong, doesn't it? So lazy.) 'Expert' number two, Leatrice Eiseman, Director of the Pantone Colour Institute, was wheeled out to give her tuppence worth on the subject, and claimed that, 'women are attracted to men wearing the colour blue'. Apparently, a guy who frequently wears blue is 'stable, faithful and always there'. Lisa developed this a little further: 'The blue guy is apparently, a fabulous candidate for a long-term relationship—someone who's dependable, monogamous and can match his own clothes.' Again, I must disagree. I have, in my modest wardrobe quite a number of blue/navy garments and wear them frequently, and have never yet found them to be possessed of pheromone-like qualities.

For ladies, of all colours to wear, 'red is the most sensual'. Leatrice added a note of caution though: 'Red is the color of sex and power', which Lisa kindly developed: 'Red adds an element of excitement and attracts two types of men—men interested in sex, and men attracted to powerful women. Sure, you'll probably have to fend off a lot of freaks, but you could also end up attracting a guy that isn't threatened by the fact that you make a bigger salary'. Astonishing, isn't it?

Number three on the list of tips for ladies was body language, and how to use it effectively to make themselves more approachable. Expert number three that Lisa called upon was none other than Patti Wood, a 'nationally respected body language expert and professional speaker'. Patti said girls who want to appear approachable targets should not take up too much space. At first I thought she was suggesting that if you were fat you shouldn't go out, but no, what she was saying was: 'we are strong women, but remember, we're trying to get a man to come over and talk to us', adding that, 'you have to show you have room for someone else in your life'. (Now that I think about it, these tips are fraught with danger: suppose you're standing in the middle of the room, wearing a cheeky red ensemble, not taking up too much space, yeah? From my reading of things, it's entirely possible that you'd come across as an attention-seeking dominatrix with a penchant for group sex. Still, it takes all sorts.) But wait, we weren't done yet—apparently there was one more thing girls were gonna have to cram into their purses before going out on the pull: a ruler. Patti said, 'to be very approachable, women should stand with their feet no farther than 6 inches apart with toes pointed slightly inward.' Complicated business this, isn't it?

As far as advice for men went, appearing more dominant was what worked, and it appeared that I'd need a ruler too, but a bigger one than that required by the ladies, because I would have to stand with my feet 6-10 inches apart, and toes pointing outward. So it was a maximum spread of 6 inches for the ladies, with toes pointing inwards, and for me, I could go as far as 10 inches apart with toes pointing outwards. I see, I see. Very interesting. Oh, and I should feel comfortable taking up 'some space' according to Lisa: apparently it's cool for a guy but not for a girl.

Fourth on the list was the old reliable—the smile, with our contributing sage, Patti Wood, soberly pointing out that 'the smile is the international signal of friendliness'. Never knew that.

Finally, last on the list is the whole issue of scents. That's s-c-e-n-t-s and not s-e-n-s-e though, so there was still more rubbish to wade through. Evidently, we men 'associate the scents of cinnamon and vanilla with love', so Lisa suggested that 'to make the scents work for you, try baking some ready-made cinnamon rolls about an hour before your date arrives, or, wear a cinnamon-vanilla scented perfume (there's a fabulous one called 'Man Magnet' available at *stopgettingdumped.com*).'

Can you get over this shit? Show me a man who can actually identify cinnamon and vanilla extracts in a woman's perfume and I'll show you a man who is looking for a man, not a woman. Another expert was wheeled out to support the cinnamon/vanilla theory: Laura Davimes, an 'aromatherapy and herb expert', claims that 'certain aromatic plants exude oils similar to our own sexual secretions or pheromones. Wearing cinnamon/vanilla blends increases the presence of pheromone-like substances and dramatically increases attraction.' For men, the advice was to get some liquorice, which according to a 'recent study' was a real turn on for the ladies. Can't argue with a rock solid source like a 'recent study', can you? I wondered how many sugared-up hyperactive six-year-olds were in that focus group.

And so. After an hour of intense meditation with my pan pipes CD, I eventually regained the will to live, and after making a note to buy a blue shirt, a ruler, and a kilo of Bassett's liquorice allsorts, I soldiered on.

One of the more credible looking singles websites that I came across was called DatingDirect.com. It claimed to be the biggest of its kind in the United Kingdom with loads of new members joining every day, blah, blah, blah, so I signed up for the crack. After paying the good-value sum of €29.99 to secure membership of the site for three months, I had to write a profile of myself, outlining what I had to offer prospective females and what kind of 'special someone' I was looking for. After much deliberation, here's what I came up with:

Hi there,

I am 34, Irish, single, currently living in Dublin, bereft of irksome facial tics and virtually insolvent as a result of a disastrous but highly enjoyable foray into the world of independent feature-film production. I love reading epic novels on deserted sunny beaches, going to the movies (except those originating in Hollywood), and am consumed by the arts in general. On the physical side of things, suffice to say that I am not embarrassing to be seen with in public. In fact, on a good day, I have previously been described as 'cute', something four independent parties can attest to if so required. I am curmudgeonly in an ultimately endearing way, allergic to cooking, gardening, doing things I don't want to do, and working too hard in general.

I am also eternally optimistic, something clearly evidenced by the fact that I remain hopeful that there is somebody out there who would find what I have going for me worth the effort involved in deducing what exactly it is I have going for me. I would like to meet an attractive, confident, modern woman aged between 30 and 40 who doesn't necessarily see giving birth and owning half a house worth in excess of £500,000 as the epitome of self-actualisation. For the sixteen or so of you that may be out there, I would like to think that a good time could be had by all should we meet up.

What do you reckon? Not too bad really, sure it's not? Covered all the salient points, I think. Bound to get a truckload of e-mails once the word got out.

I had to wait twenty-four hours for my details to be posted on the site, so I decided to familiarise myself with all the features offered to me as a fully paid-up member. The search facility was quite good, in that you were allowed to specify up to three different geographical areas from whence to choose your prospects. Very comprehensive it was too, with a complete listing of all the counties in Ireland displayed as secondary or tertiary options if you chose it as your primary search location. Given its accessibility and broad familiarity, I chose Greater London as my only search area.

The search facility also allowed one to specify any manner of requirements in relation to potential targets, so I first specified females from an age group approximating my own. (Don't know if it's a sign of old age or not, but the battle between young-healthy-libido-with-potentially-limited-capacity-for-incisive-discourse-on-a-broad-range-of-matters and the notably-more-mature-and-well-informed-view-of-the-world-somewhat-offset-by-pessimistic-outlook-and-diminished-appetite-for-exploration-of-outer-boundaries-of-sensual-pleasure was won by the latter.) After specifying females of single status with no children, I relaxed the parameters of my search field, opting for 'doesn't matter' in relation to areas such as religion, smoking, occupation, sexual proclivities—sorry, scratch that, different site—interests and the like.

I hit the search button and lo and behold, 127 results were returned for my attention. With photos attached as well, obviously— I had most definitely requested only to be presented with candidates that had uploaded photos to the site. You may feel that was rather superficial of me, and maybe it was, but that's the way it goes. You have to separate the wheat from the chaff at some stage, and if someone is either technically incapable of uploading their photo to the World Wide Web or reluctant to do so on account of how harshly they may be judged by others, then I have no desire to get to know them.

Impressed by the physical attributes of the ladies before me, I started clicking on a few of the profiles to see what the candidates had to say for themselves. A good number of them had presented themselves as wannabe Miss Worlds, saying they just wanted to meet a nice guy who had a good sense of humour, was well balanced, looking to settle down, make babies and what have you.

They were, for the most part, total honeys it has to be said, but I got the feeling that a large number of them were the type of woman who would eventually compromise everything they said was important to them in their profiles if they came across a perfectly pleasant and introverted merchant banker called Rupert, whose daddy just happened to own half of Gloucestershire.

Many others had pretty vague personal descriptions listed, no doubt on the mark and genuine enough but very few of them really jumped out at me, in terms of what they had to say about themselves or even the way they said it. And so I went purely on looks on an initial basis, taking the benefit-of-the-doubt thing to new heights rather rapidly and somehow deluding myself into thinking that these beautiful women would be interested in what I had to offer. The result was that, within about an hour I had added a bevy of beauties to my 'favourites' folder. A quick glance through it and the photos attached would suggest it was the property of some legendary porno film casting agent.

Then I realised that there was little point in me continuing to compile my list of exotic beauties resident across the water if they couldn't see me. A call was made and Paul arrived over the next day, 5 megapixel digital camera in hand, to do the necessary. After shaving and brushing my recently cropped head of distinguished, i.e. greying, hair, a crisp white shirt (didn't have a clean blue one on the day), and smart black jumper were donned. The absence of a satisfactory backdrop indoors forced us outside, where finally, under the light of a mercifully fine day and in front of a tree of some description, a selection of photographs was taken.[2] After much deliberation, an inoffensive and suitably pensive headshot of *moi* was finally selected and uploaded to the site.

The following night, bemoaning the fact that it took 72 hours for photos to be vetted and posted on the site, I decided to send a few messages to some of the women I had added to my little black favourites folder, to test the water and what not. As time was pressing on and I had a DVD to watch, I settled on a short generic message just saying 'hi' and how attractively they came across in

2. Paul's 'Come on, give it to me' exhortations did, at times, verge uncomfortably on the homoerotic, it has to be said.

their profiles, and that I would have a photo uploaded in a couple of days' time and hoped to chat to them again later on. That kind of thing. A couple of minutes cutting and pasting later and I was done. Messages sent. To Rebeccca. To Tayo. To Kate. To Karen. To Leah. To Susan. To Alex. To Isabella. To Jane. And to Linda. Oh, and to Lucy. Couldn't not send it to Lucy. Satisfied with a job well done, a bottle of Sancerre was opened and I watched my film.[3]

The next day was Wednesday, which meant dinner in a friend's house, which was not to be missed at any cost. Apart from the chat and the bit of crack which were central to the evening's proceedings, the food served up to me on these occasions was a real treat, particularly since I can't cook and have absolutely no desire to learn how to cook.

He did all the cooking, she bundled their two very pleasant small children upstairs to bed, and we enjoyed our food. We men then repaired to the back garden for a smoke and wifey cleared up.[4] Great system really. Anyway, after dinner my friend's wife informed me that she had read an article in *Vogue* magazine about one woman's online dating experience and suggested that I take it home with me and have a read of it, get to know about how things worked on the other side. I agreed, and proceeded to tell them about how things were going on my side. As only married people can, they snuggled in close together on the two-seater sofa and tried really hard not to crack up laughing as I explained to them the workings

---

3. *Lantana* was the film in question, in case you're interested. Great movie. Well worth a look.

4. You might suggest that I offer to help clearing up by way of showing my appreciation for the meal just served up to me, and you'd be right, I should. I did think about it once for a minute or so, but decided against it, reasoning that even if I wasn't there to regale them with the latest tragic episode of my personal life, they'd be eating the exact same meal. And agreement was reached early on in their now seven-year-old marriage that he would do all the grocery shopping and cooking and that she would never complain about how long it took to marinade a loin of pork or what have you and do all the clearing up afterwards. Domestic harmony is a difficult thing to achieve and I felt it was best not to meddle in matters where a happy equilibrium had been reached.

of the site, my basis of selection and my multi-pronged approach in relation to opening up the lines of communication.

Curiously, for two people who can rarely agree on any given topic without the intervention of UN-sponsored talks, they both instantly agreed that I ought to be wary of respondents who got back to me very quickly. When asked to clarify their position further, they did that terribly annoying and quite frankly rather gay, non-verbal communication thing that so many married people do—all interlocking fingers, rolling eyes, and lolling heads—and smiled at me sweetly, amazed at how little I seemed to know about matters of courtship. They went on to patiently explain that any woman who replied within twenty-four hours to a message sent by a guy who had no photo as yet visible on the site had to be, without question, a complete loon, utterly desperate to meet Mr He'll Do. I found their argument seriously flawed naturally, and tried to reason with them in a logical fashion. As skipper of the good ship *Benefit of the Doubt*, the way I saw it, a woman who received my message would no doubt at least click onto my page to read my profile. Suitably enthralled by my urbane wit and self-deprecatory manner, she would feel compelled to reply with an opening salvo of her own, and things would progress from there. This, I added, was not the action of some pathetic Bridget Jones clone who yearned for nothing more than the day she could at last drag her catatonically compliant married man along to M&S to dress him up like a live action doll with no mind of his own, but was more reflective of the actions of a progressive and confident modern woman who recognised a good thing when it came along.

A hushed silence followed as Darby and Joan silently reassessed my IQ. Thankfully, a minute later, the increasingly uneasy quiet was shattered by the spine-tingling roars of one of their children, demanding to know what was going on in the living room that they were not privy to. A quick row then ensued between the model parents to decide who should quell the revolt upstairs, which was gathering momentum, the screams of child number one having by now woken child number two, who, quite logically for someone with the cognitive capacity of a two-year-old, saw no need to consult her sibling as to the grounds for the insurgency before joining in with her own mezzo-soprano contribution. Each 'adult' party trotted out one by one their list of accomplishments for the day, successively raising the other in an effort to be recognised as the better parent and therefore entitled to keep the sofa warm whilst the other attended to the wanton destruction and dirty protests proceeding at full tilt upstairs.

Wifey eventually capitulated and as she stampeded upstairs to do the necessary, I took my leave and headed home. Booted up the computer for the crack and to my great joy discovered that I had nine new messages. A closer look however, revealed that they were merely messages from the DatingDirect central server to let me know that some of the recipients had read the message I had dispatched the previous day. Lively ladies, it had to be said, on the ball, checking their inboxes regularly. Best give them a little while to allow them time to compose a suitably gregarious reply.

Oh, but what was this in the subject bar of the last mail? Not 'Karen has *read* your message' like the rest of them, but 'Karen has *replied* to your message'. What to do? Keen as I was to log onto the site and read the mail in question, my doing so would have triggered the sending of another mail to Karen saying, 'Donal has read your message', which in turn would no doubt cause her to have a sleepless night were I not to respond immediately. And what would Darby and Joan have to say about the mental stability of a woman who replied to an unsolicited e-mail from a complete stranger within a matter of hours, I wondered?

Sod it, maybe I'll just open it and see what it says? Probably very tame and vague, it being her opening gambit: No matter, get a flavour of what she's like anyway. After all, you can only surmise so much from a picture. Yeah. Clickety-click. Let's see what we have.

Hi Donal,

Thanks for the message. It's so great that you live in Ireland, I love it there! Especially Dublin, spent last New Year's there, had such a laugh. Your profile is so well written, you seem to have had a very interesting life. Lucky you, not having to commute every

48

day to some boring office. Having said that, I do quite like my job actually—I work as a fundraiser for a non-profit organisation. I used to live in London and worked really hard in marketing for a couple of years, but packed it in and took my foot off the pedal a little as other things took priority. So that's a little about me, hope to hear from you soon.

Bye for now,
Karen

The deranged ramblings of a 'loon'? I think not. Seemed like a perfectly pleasant woman to me. Liked my profile too. Okay, if you really wanted to read between the lines, the foot-off-the-pedal/ other-things-taking-priority bit might reasonably have been cause for some concern, suggestive as it was of a woman on the hunt for Mr Right. Which is fair enough, I supposed. She was 36 after all— she'd want to get a move on if she wanted to have kids. Thought I'd sleep on it and reply to her tomorrow.

——

Tell you something. Being an apprentice womaniser isn't all it's cracked up to be. Takes up a huge amount of your time, what with logging onto sites, checking inboxes, editing profiles, uploading photos, keeping track of who you're communicating with, checking their profiles to see what way you should play it with them . . . Just as well I didn't have a job.

By the end of April I was going full tilt on a number of fronts. I joined another dating site called Anotherfriend.com. Pathetic name, I know, but there you go, it was actually quite good.[5] It's

5. Didn't have to write too detailed a profile for this one, just answer a load of basic questions about myself, like, age (34), location (kitchen), height (5'10"), weight (too much), hair colour (greying brown), education (firm believer in it), what kind of car I drive (a piece of shit), what my occupation is (don't have one), salary (not enough), star sign (complete rubbish) . . . You get the idea. Then you're asked to describe yourself a bit. I went for:

based in Ireland, but is not exclusively for Irish people, although they do comprise the majority of people on it. I suppose you could say it's aimed at people with an interest in all things Irish. You've seen one dating site, you've seen them all to a certain extent, but this one has a nice little feature on it where you can send someone an electronic 'wink' if they catch your eye. So you don't get a message, just notification that so-and-so had a look at your profile and thought you were all right. It's up to you to wink back or take the initiative and send them an opening message. Great idea it is too, I reckon. Let's say you're in a bar and you spot an attractive woman sitting at the table across from you with a group of her friends. However much you might want to talk to her, approaching her table is not without its risks. She could tell you to sod off, leaving you to walk back to your mates like a tit. She could be a lesbian. She could be married. She could be involved with someone. You just don't know. But if a woman registered on a dating site sends you an electronic wink, I think it's safe to say that she's interested in being approached. And most definitely not a lesbian. (Unless you're really lucky.) So anyway, that's the winking thing. I'm pleased to report that in the six days I was a member of the site, my profile was viewed 43 times (excluding the six times I viewed it myself. Not on a narcissistic level you understand, merely to ensure that my personal data had been correctly displayed), and I had received three winks. From three different women.

And I was scouring the personal ads in the paper. I found a few in it one Friday which sounded interesting enough, from people who seemed like they were up for actually having a laugh for a couple of years before settling into the humdrum suburban thing. I listened to a few of the messages and decided to leave one of my own with a young lady by the name of Lisa. Lisa was 30, she loved

5. contd

> *Single, not embarrassing to be seen with in public. No interest in index-linked pensions, tracker mortgages or kids. Greatest achievement to date is not having worn a tie in ten years. Hate working, like drinking, smoking, having a laugh, especially on a Tuesday afternoon when the rest of the world is sitting at a desk.*

I know, I know. It is rather good.

going to the cinema, and cooking (fine by me—if it's put in front of me I'll eat it). She also liked to keep fit by swimming and riding regularly. (Horses, you degenerate.) She lived in Dublin, which was cool logistically, and worked in IT, whatever that entails these days. She sounded all right, on a dipping-your-toe-in-the-water kind of level, so I left her a jolly enough sounding message about how great I am and how well I reckon we'd both get on, what with us having so much in common. Okay—there was an element of spin there. Big deal.

Also, after finally getting my photo 'cleared' on decency grounds by the site police at DatingDirect, my mug was now there for all to see, and I established relations with a couple of the women registered on the site, although things were on a strictly casual level. And I'm talking about things from my point of view here— the women in question could very well have been totally besotted with me, sobbing themselves to sleep every night, despairing of the Irish Sea that lay between us, hoping against hope that some day very soon they would be able to see me in the flesh, as it were. Or not. Whatever.

Some of them didn't even reply to my cheeky little opening gambit either, which I found most unsettling—no point in having the body of a Greek goddess if common courtesy was lacking I thought. I was going to delete them from my favourites folder on a point of principle, but then I discovered that the site offered people the facility to check to see who had added their profile to their list of favourites, and so decided to delete my entire listing straight away. Didn't want any of them getting big heads thinking they were only fantastic. Especially seeing as how none of them had added me to their list of favourites, something I obviously checked out as soon as I discovered it was possible to do so.

So I was down to mailing three of them—Karen, Rebecca and Jane—which out of a starting batch of eleven wasn't too bad I think—a 27.27 per cent hit rate for the statistically minded amongst you. Not necessarily the three I would *most* like to have opened lines of communication with, if I'm to be completely honest with you, but three pleasant enough women nonetheless. I did know that technically, given the relative paucity of communication that had passed between us thus far, I should have retained an open mind, but it was proving hard to do. Judging from the quality of their correspondence, I was in no rush to clock up another couple of hundred on the plastic schlepping over to London for a date just yet. Having said that, if I could I swing it so that I could do lunch with one of them, the least likely prospect, say, an early dinner with another, the number two candidate, and then a few drinks and a late movie with the main contender, that'd be pretty cool, I figured. Perfectly legitimate behaviour as well, given my previously adopted exclusivity rule. Three hits in the one day, and I could be back home *chez moi* by lunchtime Sunday. Be a right bit of crack as well. Probably would never happen though. Still, I filed it away for future reference—you never know.

Anyway, the really big news, the mega news from around then, was that I was in love. Smitten. Absolutely smitten. The lucky woman's name was Daisy Garnett. Guess where I came across her? No. Guess again. No. Guess again. No. Again. No; God you're thick. She was the one who wrote the article in *Vogue*, stupid. About being single and her online dating experience. I'd forgotten all about the magazine to be honest with you, until I was stuck in the most heinous traffic jam known to mankind one day on the way home from town. I tried a bit of chanting and some crystal work, but to no avail, I was totally stressed and about to crack up altogether when I caught sight of the magazine on the back seat. I'd no intention of reading an article obviously, just reckoned I'd do a quick nipple count in the hope that it would take my mind off the incontrovertible fact that the pensioners shuffling along the pavement were progressing at a greater speed than I was. So there I was, happily flicking through the pages of the magazine (11 separate sightings so far, including advertisements), when I came across the article about the whole online dating thing. I started reading it as I inched along the riverside and got so engrossed in it that I had to pull over to give it my full attention.

I spent the next hour reading Ms Garnett's article and have to say that by the time I was halfway through it I knew that she was th-

05

Sorry for cutting you off like that, but I felt that Daisy deserved a chapter of her own. And with good reason too, I'm sure you'll agree as we move on. So, like I was saying, I knew that she was the one for me. You know the way you read an article or a book by someone and you totally buy into everything they say? Fiction or non-fiction, you're there nodding your head as you're going along, agreeing with the author or principal character out loud, or empathising with them and the situations they find themselves in? And then you get to the end of the article or whatever and you're dying to get your hands on some more information about the author, perhaps naively thinking you'd have loads in common with them and that they'd love you to be their new mate? Or even just to see what they looked like, to see if it matched the image of them you've already built up in your head for no good reason? You do? Good, because that's exactly the way I felt about Daisy as soon as I finished the article. Imagine my elation then, when I discovered on the contributors' page a photo of none other than Ms Daisy Garnett!

And guess what? She looked exactly as I imagined she would. Clothed, of course. Honestly, she did. I knew she'd have blonde hair. I knew it would be short and kind of wispy and would need a clip of some sort in it or else she'd be blowing it out of her eyes all day the way women with short hair and no clips do, which is something I find terribly sexy. Women pursing their lower lip and blowing upwards in a north-easterly or north-westerly direction, depending on which side they part their hair, taking the opportunity to flutter their eyes for a second as they do so? God, that freaks me out so it does.

So. There she was. Quite apart from brilliantly conveying Daisy's own natural, radiant beauty and winning personality, what I liked about the photo was the fact that it had obviously been taken in a very natural setting. (A foreign locale too, I'd venture.) No posed, studio-lit bullshit, just Daisy sitting at a table with some friends, the debris of a no-doubt-heartily enjoyed meal surrounding them. She'd turned to her left to listen to what the person next to her was saying, giving them her full attention, her piercing blue eyes drilling into their core, as if on a mission to seek out supporting information which she could use to agree with whatever was being said to her. Which you know she wants to, because that's the kind of girl she is—supportive, and open, and all into consensus building and what have you. (But a woman of integrity no less, a woman who would feel honour bound to disagree wholeheartedly with you if you said something that upset her or offended her.)

And then there was the little bio beside the photo as well, which had a few snippets of information about her. She'd sailed across the Atlantic Ocean. She'd ridden a camel across the Syrian Desert. She loved to dance, went out every night, was, by her own admission, 'messy in appearance' and yet 'obsessively tidy at home'. She was mad about her sisters, a voracious reader, and found doing a spot of needlepoint or sipping a glass of Scotch a great way to relax. And she was half Irish.

'Oh, God, she's a vision. To look at a face like that with love and have love returned—what would that be like?'[1]

Now this, this was what I was looking for: a woman who quite literally assaulted my every sense, a woman who, without knowing

1. This great line was humbly lifted from Jonathan Ames' brilliant book *What's Not To Love?—The Adventures of a Mildly Perverted Young Writer*. Hilarious stuff altogether.

it herself, demanded that I pay attention to her and react to her. And we'd so much in common too! Well maybe that was a bit wide of the mark. I haven't actually sailed across the Atlantic Ocean. I have however sailed, sorry, been *on* a boat which, competently crewed by a friend of mine and his father, sailed, from Clontarf in North Dublin to Bray in County Wicklow, which must be at least 15 miles. (Must work out the nautical mile equivalent actually, see if it sounds more impressive expressed that way. Sailing folk probably expect it as well—wouldn't want to slip up if I were pressed on the issue.) And fair enough, I haven't ridden a camel across the Syrian Desert, or anywhere else for that matter. I don't dance, and I go out so rarely that such nights are the focus of an insane amount of attention in the weeks preceding them, and almost unfailingly, are the subject of much morose scrutiny afterwards as I doggedly seek out explanations as to why a simple bite to eat and a few drinks in an unremarkable venue with people I've known for years did not turn out to be the highlight of my year to date.

I am quite messy in my appearance though, if that counts for anything. And I also keep my house very tidy. Admittedly my needlepoint technique isn't all that it should be, and I'd rather a glass of white wine to a glass of Scotch any day. I am however, most definitely a voracious reader, and currently have a reading list of some 67 books to get through.[2] And, I can actually trump Ms Garnett's achievement in one particular category: where she is merely half-Irish, I am 100 per cent Irish. (It's not something I have historically considered to be an achievement in itself, and nor would I list it as such on a CV were I ever unfortunate enough to have compile one in the future, but if Daisy saw fit to append her half-Irish status to her bite-sized bullet-pointed bio on the contributors page of *Vogue*, then I saw no good reason why I shouldn't bring my Irish nationality to her attention.)

By now the traffic had all but disappeared and I sped home to

2. I am, I must confess, somewhat addicted to buying books, with the result that at any given time, I could be reading up to four concurrently in an effort to get through the towering cityscape of books that wobble precariously atop my otherwise perfectly maintained and alphabetically organised bookcase, which itself cannot accommodate any more volumes.

compose my letter to Daisy—a crucial piece of correspondence and no mistake, one that demanded to be crafted with great care and attention. Did a quick Google search on her of course, just to gather some more background information on her. Found out that she is the daughter of Polly Devlin, a British writer of some note, and that one of her much-adored and overly talked-about sisters was one Bay Garnett, founder of a very hip New York-based magazine called *Cheap Date*. As well as the *Vogue* gig, Daisy also paid her way writing feature articles for *The Daily Telegraph* and *The Guardian*, and had interviewed such luminaries as P Diddy and Cate Blanchett, to name but two. Heaps more too; Google is such a great resource[3]—it felt like I'd known her for years.

And so I started to compose my letter to Daisy. A mere two and a half hours later I was done and the resulting final draft is reproduced (overleaf) for your consideration:

3. Mildly amusing and totally unrelated anecdote, as are most of these footnotes. (Unrelated that is; not necessarily amusing, mildly or otherwise.) In search of a new outlet for my creative urges, I signed up for a 26-week-long bronze casting evening course a couple of years ago. During a break on the first night I struck up a conversation with this rather intense looking chap. His tone was rather caustic and his manner terribly pass-remarkable so naturally we got on famously. After summarily dismissing the artistic merits of our fellow classmates, simply because our faulty default settings predisposed us to do so, we exchanged names and brief potted bios, during the course of which I made mention of a rather crap feature film I had produced and the title of my first book, which had been recently published. The following week I was greeted by this same chap in a markedly different manner, verging on the deferential. During our break he confessed that he had 'googled' me during the week and was amazed at how prolific an artist I was. I shrugged nonchalantly, dismissed the film as the piece of shit it was, and expressed high hopes for the book. He went on to make mention of a number of artistic achievements attributed to Donal Ruane, none of which I could remember, principally because they weren't my achievements. Turned out, there was some arty dude based in Slovenia or somewhere like that with the same name as yours truly and my new acquaintance had rather flatteringly come to the conclusion that he and I were the same person. That is, he was me, and by extension, his artistic achievements were mine also. (There was only one Daisy Garnett though, have no fear.)

Hi Daisy,

I know you like your Scotch, but seeing as how you're half Irish, I thought a bottle of Irish whiskey would best suit the occasion of my formal declaration of you as one hell of a girl.

Whilst having dinner at a friend's house recently, I read your excellent feature in Vogue *detailing your online dating odyssey, and have to say that halfway through I was sincerely hoping that none of your dates would amount to anything of any note. Not because I'm wilful you understand, but simply because I found you incredibly attractive and am—however naïvely—convinced we would enjoy each other's company.*

Short of 'pitching' directly for the invaluable Daisy Garnett account at this early stage, for your information, let me just say that I am 34 years old, bereft of irksome facial tics, virtually insolvent as a result of a disastrous but enjoyable foray into the world of independent film production, somewhat delusional in that I am currently a full-time writer, not embarrassing to be seen with in public, consumed by the arts in general, curmudgeonly in an endearing way, and eternally hopeful that somewhere beyond these shores lies somebody fantastic who would find what I have going for me worth the effort involved in ascertaining what exactly it is that I have going for me.

And so, I hope that if things don't progress too far with your acquaintance from New York, you might consider allowing me to buy you dinner sometime. (Next week is good for me.)

All the best,
Donal

I know, I know. It's really quite something. As you will have gathered from the opening line above, my letter was not dispatched to Ms Daisy Garnett, Commissioning Editor, *Vogue*, Vogue House, Hanover Square, London W1S 1HA on its own. Oh, no. The letter was accompanied by a rather splendid bottle of 16-year-old Bushmills Irish whiskey, which itself was beautifully presented in an aged wooden box and nestling on a bed of straw. How spectacular is that? Bound to get a date with her, at the very least. As far as I could discern from the article in the magazine, she was single at the outset of her little online odyssey, had a number of assignations with a variety of men, none of whom seemed to really rock her world, and she wrapped up the article by stating that she was currently seeing a chap she used to know when she lived in New York, who she had come across on Friendster.com. They'd only been on four dates though, so it was hardly serious. And I'd bet my bottom dollar, which I was rapidly approaching, that he had never bestowed on her a gift of such thoughtfulness as mine, so I thought that more than cancelled out the fact that he actually knew her and had met her in person, lucky bastard that he was. And, of course, the fact that it was a bottle of premium Irish whiskey as opposed to a bottle of Scotch whiskey would convey to Daisy that I, the bestower, was myself 100 per cent Irish. And of a premium calibre too, naturally.

——

My gift and letter were dispatched by courier the following day, which was a Wednesday, so, all going to plan, the beautifully packaged surprise would land on Ms Garnett's desk in London no later than the following Monday. Assuming she was in the country and not off globetrotting, interviewing some celebrity or what have you, I expected to hear from her no later than the Wednesday of the following week. Any earlier and she might fear she was showing her hand too quickly (assuming obviously, that she was as enraptured with the gift and the contents of the letter to the degree I hoped). Any later and it would be plain bad manners, really; and I was satisfied that she was from good stock, and that the timely acknowledgment of gifts received was something that would have been instilled in her as a child.

I would also venture that the most likely medium she would use to convey her heartfelt thanks to me would be e-mail.[4] Why so?

4. I did include in the letter all my correspondence details—postal address, mobile telephone number and e-mail address—but have omitted to reproduce them here in case I bring unsolicited attention on myself from a number of the admiring females amongst you who may be reading this right now. (In much the same way as I had that very day, wholly unsolicitedly, foisted my own presence on Ms Daisy Garnett.)

Well, for a number of reasons, now that you ask. Firstly, much as there are few things as satisfying as the discovery of a handwritten note of appreciation on one's floor on a given morning, shrouded and all as it may be within a protective layer of despicable junk mail, the frequency with which such delights occur is undoubtedly waning. What with people being so busy these days, there just isn't the time to source quality notepaper, sit down at one's bureau, compose a worthy note in one draft—there's no delete/cut-and-paste facility with a fountain pen—address the matching envelope, affix the requisite stamps to the envelope and deposit it in a post box that hasn't been sealed off in order to prevent a terrorist attack.

Secondly, it's a confident and forthright woman indeed who would telephone a suitor to convey her appreciation of a gift received. Such a scenario is fraught with the potential for awkwardness, possibly even downright calamity when you think about it. The thing about mobile phones is that you just don't know what kind of situation the person you are calling may be in. They could be discommoded in some way—on the commode even—which would impinge their ability to engage with you on an enthusiastic level, thus misinforming the caller as to the true nature of their affections for them. Another thing: after the essential business of the call has been dispatched with, how long should one remain on the line chit chatting about the weather and what not? Too long and pregnant pauses could abound; not long enough and you run the risk of being either uninteresting or introverted. It's a risky business and no mistake.

No, I was sure Daisy would reply via e-mail. Apart from being the quickest and easiest option open to her, it was also the option with the least exposure attached to it. Think about it. There would be no judgement passable on her handwriting, in itself a reasonable concern, seeing as how, regardless of educational attainment, the script of your average adult these days could well be displayed as part of an exhibition of asylum art, given the rarity with which people actually do put pen to paper. Also, no judgement could be made on the basis of her cadence, a reasonable concern as well I suppose, given how quick people are to judge one another purely on the basis of accent these days. An e-mail however, can be deliberated on, rehearsed, amended and spell-checked over the course of a day until the sender is satisfied with both content and tone, and then dispatched, stampless, in an instant.

And so the wait began.

'Oh, God, she's a vision. To look at a face like that with love and have love returned—what would that be like?'

06

The day after I sent my letter and gift to Daisy I called over to Paul's house to fill him in on the big news. He was pleased with my efforts, but keen to get things moving again closer to home. He reminded me of a girl that I had met at his wedding and suggested we give it a shot.

'She's cute all right,' I said, handing the photograph back to Rachel, Paul's wife. 'I don't remember meeting her at your wedding, though.'

'Well, you would have if you'd got up off your arse and mingled a bit. That's what people do at weddings, you know? They move around from table to table and get to know people,' Rachel said matter-of-factly.

'She's a babe, Do. And she's single. Recently too,' Paul said reassuringly.

'And for some bizarre reason modern science can't quite explain, she remembers you and seems to like you,' Rachel added.

'That's understandable,' I said. 'I suppose she's a bloody account-ant as well, yeah?'

''Fraid so. She's good at it though—made manager a couple of months ago. Owns her own apartment in Rathfarnham; drives a Mini. Likes her tunes; dresses well. Big into movies—all that art-house shit you like too. It's our best option at the minute. On paper she's Premiership material. Give it a lash, and if it doesn't work out we'll move on,' Paul suggested eagerly, obviously keen for this proposed date with Louise to get the all-clear from Rachel, a work colleague of Louise's.

Rachel, for her part, had seemed agreeable to the idea at first, but now that a 'Do-you-want-to-dance-with-my-friend'-type phone call loomed on the horizon, appeared to be having second thoughts. She said nothing for a minute and edged her massive frame towards the edge of the sofa, so as to be able to lever herself upwards. God, she really was huge—I couldn't understand how she could be happy like that.

'If you make a mess of this, I'll kill you,' she said sternly to me as she walked, or wobbled, towards the kitchen.

'Come on, Rachel, what's that supposed to mean? If we click, we click, that's all there is to it,' I answered defensively. 'So, when are you taking your maternity leave, next week or the week after?' I continued, eager to keep things on track.

'This Friday actually, why?' she asked, perhaps a tad suspiciously, as she filled the kettle.

'Well,' Paul replied, 'we were thinking that maybe that'd be the best time for us all to go for a little drink, you know? Get this pair reacquainted and then leave them to it. If things don't pan out, it's no biggie—you'll be finished up for six months, so there'll be no stress, you know?'

'Yeah, I suppose you're right,' Rachel agreed, a little less enthusiastically than I would have liked.

'You making coffee, Rach?' Paul called.

'Yeah. Do you want one?'

'Lovely. Thanks, hon. And a Toffee Crisp as well, while you're up,' he said affectionately. 'Game on,' he said, winking at me before returning his attention to the two matches he was watching simultaneously on his new 42-inch TV.

———

'She farted?' Rachel asked me again in disbelief when I called over for the 'post-match analysis' Paul had suggested.

'Swear to God. She farted,' I repeated calmly.

Paul slumped back pensively into the depths of his La-Z-Boy recliner.

'That's bad form, isn't it, Rach?' he said sincerely, muting the sound on the TV.

'What are you like?' she muttered exasperatedly, addressing the two of us from her supine position on the sofa. 'What's that got to do with anything?'

'Well, not a lot, at the end of the day I suppose,' I said, 'but it was a little odd—I've never actually heard a girl fart before, to be honest with you.'

'And you thought it would be a good thing to talk about, yeah? My God, you really are an idiot,' she said admonishingly. 'I don't know why I ever agreed to this whole thing in the first place. I was mortified when she told me that you actually *brought it up.*'

'I was only having a laugh with her. She didn't need to react like that. She must be a bit up-tight, is she?'

'No, she is not up-tight. She's an intelligent, educated professional used to dating men with a little more tact and politeness than you can obviously muster up,' Rachel chided.

'Ah, now, fair's fair, Rachel. She's a bit of a square, really,' Paul said, interceding on my behalf. 'Do was doing all the running, by the sounds of it . . .'

'If you thought she was a square, then why were you so keen to set them up last week?'

'I just wanted to get the ball rolling, you know? How was I supposed to know she was gonna fart? Right there in the restaurant, yeah?'

'Yeah. I couldn't believe it,' I continued. 'We were standing just in the door waiting for our table. We'd only had the one quick drink before—because she was late I might add—and the conversation wasn't really flowing, you know? I think she was a little nervous maybe. So there we are, waiting to be seated, and all of a sudden, I heard this little pop. Well, more like a quick succession of little pops, really. I wasn't that pushed about it, but when I looked at her, she turned away. I could tell she was embarrassed— she was puce—so I thought I'd make light of the whole thing, you know? Just trying to help her out, like. So I said, "Better out than in", and smiled. That was it.'

'Oh, that's classic,' Paul said, not able to contain his laughter any more. 'And what did she say? Was there a bit of a hum off her?'

'No, not that I got anyway. We were at the door so she had the wind at her back as well I suppose. It was more the sound of it really—kind of like a car running out of petrol or something . . . She didn't say anything. Pretended she didn't hear me, and then as soon as we got our table, she went off to the loo. And when she came back, she was a bit sniffy, you know? Like I'd said she was fat or something. It was a bit childish of her, I thought . . .'

'*A bit childish of her*? Are you out of your mind?' Rachel said loudly, rubbing her big belly for added effect. 'She thinks you're a complete moron and never wants to see you again.'

'That's a bit rich. Who says I want to see her again? She's not up to much anyway. That accent would get on your wick after a while too.'

'And was there any action afterwards?' Paul asked bluntly.

'You kidding me? She didn't even want a coffee—said she was tired—so we split and I got her a taxi. That was it. Waste of time.'

07

After the disastrous episode with the flatulence-prone Louise I decided to focus my attention on my international prospects for a while and see what came of that. Sad thing was though, things weren't looking too good for the ladies I had been fraternising with on the DatingDirect site now that Daisy was in the frame. You see, when I get an idea into my head that I want something to happen, that's pretty much it—everything else gets shoved to one side as I doggedly pursue that one goal. And so now, as my pursuance of Daisy took over my life, not only would it leave me with less time to consort with these other ladies, my actual inclination to do so would wane considerably as well—I mean how could any of them stack up against Daisy? They were all lovely in their own way I'm sure, but they just didn't have that indefinable something that I knew Daisy had, and that I know I need in a woman if things are going to go anywhere at all.

Every woman has a certain indefinable something all right, don't get me wrong. That's how they all end up married: a guy will see one particular thing in a woman that does something for him alone and vice versa and it's happy ever after. But, the certain indefinable something (hereinafter referred to as CIS), that I'm after, well, that's a much more elusive thing altogether. I've only ever actually met one woman before who had it. She was quite something, but our timing was wrong. At least hers was; I would have married her two weeks after meeting her, but alas, it was not to be. (Not then anyway—I still have her details filed away for future reference should I ever feel compelled to give it another shot.) And though there have been a few close calls down through the years, Daisy is pretty much only the second woman I have ever met who has that particular cis that I want and need. And in her case, I hadn't even *met* her yet, so it must have been the real deal if she could knock me out like that from the pages of a magazine.

Still, trying not to get too carried away with myself, I thought it best to hedge my bets and keep up with a few of the other prospects I had been incubating. The sad news was that the Karen thing went by the wayside pretty quickly. I know, I know—it'd be hard for her and the nights would seem endless, but it was for the best. We were mailing each other for a week or so and it was all very pleasant and what have you, but I didn't really think there was anything in the sub-text of her mails, never mind the text itself, that suggested to me that there was something to be followed through with, do you know what I mean?

I'm not saying I expect a woman to tell me that she loves me when she's never met me before, in fact that'd be the last thing I'd want to hear from someone. (Apart from Daisy, obviously.) But all the same, I do think that—even making allowances for the fact that people may understandably have their guard up initially when they are corresponding with somebody new, even if the chosen medium for said correspondence is one as sterile as e-mail—it should be clear to both parties pretty early on whether there is a fundamental connection there worth building on. And I have to say, that even after swapping just a few mails with Karen, I knew there wasn't. Not from my perspective, anyway. Poor thing, she could have been mad about me from the get go, you never know. Or else maybe she was just taking a longer-term view of things and not judging too much in the very early days. Maybe that's the right way to look these things, but it's not the way I'm set up to look at them.

So I decided to stop mailing her. Which may sound harsh, but really I think it was the best option open to me. The others would have involved either blocking her from sending me mails in the future, which I thought was a bit brutal—I mean it's not like I was scared of her or anything—or else writing her a big long e-mail explaining what I've just tried to explain to you. And that probably wouldn't have gone down too well either. I mean, let's face it, when someone tells you they don't feel like it's working out—after only a few e-mails and all—it's human nature to parry with one of your own, 'Well,-I-didn't-think-it-was-going-anywhere-myself,-was-going-to-mail-you-in-the-next-few-minutes-actually,-to-tell-you—as-much,-just-wanted-to-give-it-some-thought-so-as-not-to-hurt-your-feelings,-you-know,-because-I'm-fine-with-this,-I-really-am,-I'm-fine,-absolutely-fine,-but-you-know,-I-have-to-do-what's-best-for-me,-because-that's-what-I-deserve,-and-I-just-think-that-we-don't-have-anything . . .' kind of speeches.

And it's a bit childish really, I think, so I reckoned it would be just better not to reply and then she'd get the message in a couple of days or so. And who knows, she could very well have been thinking the exact same thing, and had been psyching herself up to send me a big long mail explaining why she didn't think it was going to work out. And if she had, that would have been fine by me, to be honest with you.

As for the other two I was dropping a line to, Rebecca and Jane, well, I don't know. Physically, they were undoubtedly very attractive girls—I'd give them both a six out of Daisy—but it was hard to know at this stage what exactly they were looking for. (Especially since I didn't really know what I was looking for myself—I was banking on recognising it when I saw it.) Of the two though, I much preferred Jane. To be honest, Rebecca caught my eye initially because, apart from being quite cute, she happened to live in Belgravia and I, racing ahead of myself as I oftentimes do, got to thinking that if things worked out between us, she would no doubt come with a very substantial dowry. I know, I know, it's hardly the best way to go about establishing a mutually respectful and sustainable relationship, but there you go—I got a little carried away that first night.

I have to say though, even making allowances for the possibility of Rebecca coming with a respectable dowry—quite often a matter of considerable concern to females as well when assessing the suitability of a suitor—I'm not sure we could ever come to share a lot of common ground. As I heard someone once remark on the different backgrounds he and his girlfriend came from, 'She had a pony, I had a paper round.' Rebecca worked for her father, a property developer, four days a week, taking Fridays off to 'be with' her mother,[1] who was 'living apart' from her father, as she delicately put it. Weeknights were spent working out at the gym (and the results were there to see, I might add), or relaxing at home, home being a two-bed apartment in a large house off Eaton Square that Daddy had converted into apartments some years previously, generously retaining one of them for his little princess. Weekends consisted of much shopping and socialising with friends, all of whom appeared to be similarly moneyed. To some of you, this may sound like an idyllic existence, but as far as I'm concerned, when you look past the glossy veneer of such lives, there is more often than not a gaping hole to be found, normally in the same place where most other people store their interests, passions, and thoughts. Maybe I was being unjustifiably judgemental of Rebecca at this early stage, but then again, maybe not. To wit: if her life was unblemished in any way, what was she doing on a singles website?

Jane, though, held out some promise. As our correspondence increased in frequency, the biographical details I learned cast her in quite a good light. She appeared not only to be an intelligent woman—a barrister—but also a woman with a creative leaning: a keen painter, she had just had three of her pieces selected for exhibition in a group show taking place in a small gallery off the Kings' Road.[2] And she was rather good looking, insofar as I could

1. As we grew gradually more familiar with each other and accounts of our everyday activities were exchanged in increasing detail, I took it that 'be[ing] with' her mother generally entailed Rebecca accompanying her on excursions to a number of exclusive boutiques before the pair repaired to a swanky restaurant for a very late, and very long, lunch.

2. All landscapes, painted from photographs taken whilst on a cycling holiday with her sister in Tuscany the previous summer.

tell from the jpeg image she had uploaded to the site. Another thing in Jane's favour, from my point of view at least, was that she was only 31, and consequently had not, as yet, embarked on her search for a lifelong soulmate. Also, she said she hadn't really been on the dating scene for quite some time, which led me to suspect that she would be amenable to enjoying quite a casual type of relationship.

So that was the plan—I would forge ahead and try to move things along with Rebecca and Jane, maybe get a lunch thing going or something. I'd give them some line about having to be in London on business soon, which hopefully I would be—said business relating to Ms Daisy Garnett.

Also, quite out of the blue, I got a mail one morning in the third week of May from a young lady called Vera. I have to say I was intrigued, because she wasn't one of the starlets I had appended to my porno folder that first night when I'd gone a bit mad, clicking on every foxy lady I came across. Vera's message was fairly short, and very sweet. Just a few lines, saying hello and what have you. So I clicked on her profile to have a look at what she had to say for herself. Turned out that she was 25, and lived in Russia, in a place called Ryazan, where she worked as a teacher. Very attractive woman she was too, I have to say. Not in the same utterly beguiling way that Daisy was obviously, but an undeniably attractive woman nonetheless. She was a good height. Slim. Long blonde ringlety hair cascading down over a very pretty face. Good cheekbones and what have you, and her profile was very engaging. Written in broken English—something which I happen to find quite attractive—it read like this:

> Hello!!!!!! Me call Vera. I live in city of Ryazan. I take a great interest in music, books. I want get acquainted with decent fair the man. On which it is possible will rely in a difficult minute. I hate a deceit and cowardice. I respect people, who is honour, straight line, is capable to sympathy and trust. Interests and plans during the future let try to know each other better. Please notice, I look only for the serious long attitudes. If you search only for sexual attitudes or friends on correspondence, please to not answer.

What to make of that, then? Sounded, and certainly looked, quite lovely, I think.[3] In fairness, I figured that she wanted to get out of Ryazan and hoof it down the aisle quick enough, but could you blame her? Bad and all as I make Dublin out to be, I would quickly guess that it beats Ryazan hands down, even though I've never been there. So I sent Vera back a little message saying 'hi' and asking her more about her job and what she liked to do and all that kind of thing. Not because I was thinking anything might come of it, you understand: more so because she had got in touch with me off her own bat and I didn't feel I was in any position to be that choosy. A mere two hours later, I was furnished with a reply:

> *Hello Donal,*
>
> *I am very strongly glad to receive from you the letter. I live in Russia, the city of Ryazan. I am engaged in education of children. I am the teacher. I very much love them but unfortunately I do not have children. But I hope that in the fast future I will have children. At me is growth of 173cm, my weight of 57 kgs. I do not have parents. I live by one, I like to go in theatre and cinema. I like classical music, but all depends on mood. I shall be very strongly glad if you to answer my letter. I wish to you good day!!!*
> *Your Vera*

God, she was keen! I figured that either I didn't give myself half enough credit for how attractive I am or things really must have been quite dire in Ryazan. Either way though, this one bore all the hallmarks of a banker, if you know what I mean.

'Mum, Dad, this is Vera. We're getting married.'

3. Paul thought she was 'a ride', and urged me to give the proposal due consideration. Rooting for me and all as he was, I suspect that his urging me to explore this rather unorthodox avenue stemmed partly from the fact that since his wife Rachel gave birth to a fabulously healthy bouncing baby boy the previous week (9 lbs 10 ozs), the reality of parental responsibility and marital fidelity had finally hit him, and that he knew such options were no longer a runner for him. Truth be told, he's also something of a deviant at heart and would dearly love to live vicariously through another.

Didn't know how well that'd go down, much as they kept bugging me about being single, but it was most definitely an ace in the hole if ever I needed it. And so, out of politeness more than anything else, a response was dispatched to Vera. Nothing too involved, mind—I was just being friendly.

——

If you'd asked me my opinion on the matter, I wouldn't have thought that every classroom in Ryazan was hooked up to the Internet, but when I logged onto the site again that afternoon, checking to see if I had received a message from Jane, I was somewhat surprised to see a reply from Vera, which had been sent very shortly after I had sent my previous message to her. Curiously, whatever way she had read my message, she had apparently chosen to believe that we were meant to be together, as can be evidenced from her rather long e-mail:

I am pleased to receive from you a symbol, and I hope that our correspondence in the future will develop in closer communication between us. It is my first experience in transfer with the man by means of the Internet!

Know that I should write to you now. I looked at your structure, and you have liked me, and for this reason I have decided answer to you. I am the Russian girl, never married, and without children. But I like children. I love to travel but I was not in other countries but dreamed to visit there from my childhood. Unfortunately it is too magnificent for many citizens of Russia and for me including.

I like to meet the man, who is focused on the family, who wants to frame family and to have children. All this you could know from my structure, but I am really serious in my search, and I am sure it can be. If you ask to me why I try to do it in such a way, that is new to me, then sincerely, I have the same question to you. So please, explain for me your prompting. As to me I am deeply disappointed by our men. They too much think of themselves.

And they do not think concerning anything except for presence of the entertainment and sex. Few men think to frame the large strong family or understand it correctly. I so hope that I can be with the foreign men, more serious is better also.

I love to be a lot in the nature, driving on a ski, and to sit on a coast of a lake to look at the descending of the sun, and at singing birds. It so is beautiful and romantically. I do like the romantic but is difficult to find the understanding man.

I respect people, who have honour, are straight on the line, are capable to sympathy and trust. Interests and plans for the future is good, but let us try to know each other better now. Please notice, I look only for the serious long attitudes.

I hope that you will write to me. Yes I want to find the husband that is strong. And I want to leave Russia. Please tell about you as much as possible, I very much want to learn it. I hope that our correspondence becomes a first step to closer attitude.

Vera.

Okay, a couple of points, if I may. One. What exactly constitutes a 'symbol' these days? All I did was ask her about her city, the ages of the kids she taught and what her family situation was like. Two. She'd better get a few more English lessons. What part of my admittedly rather eruditely composed profile could have lead her to conclude that I was 'focused on the family'? Three. Why should I have to explain my reasons for joining the site? She was the one looking to up sticks and get married. Four. I don't ski.

I could go on, but I thought my points were best directed at the schoolteacher herself. Better get a reply off to her post haste. In very plain English as well, lest there be any confusion—didn't want her mistaking this next message for another 'symbol' or she'd probably hand in her notice and tell all her friends she was moving to Dublin.

Hi Vera,

Thanks for your long message. I do not know if you did read my structure very closely, but I do not want to get married. I do not want to frame the family, or have the children. I think you are a

very nice woman and very pretty but I am not looking for a wife.
Not now, at this point in time. Now, I only want to go out with a
woman, to get to know them very well at first. That is all. I hope
you understand this.

  Take care,
  Donal

That should do it. Set out my stall quite clearly there, I thought—
a blind man could see what I was talking about. Didn't want to
hurt her feelings or anything, but I didn't want her getting the
wrong idea either. I was not on for framing the family. Not now,
not ever.

08

In between corresponding with Vera, I had another date—with Lisa, my IT girl, whose ad in the paper I had responded to a couple of weeks previously. As our phone calls had progressed, both in terms of their frequency and duration,[1] I had decided that,

1. The first call proper was made by me after Lisa had replied to the message I had left on her voice-mail, saying she'd like to talk. It lasted only a few minutes—quick hellos, followed by a mini Q&A session, which allowed each party the opportunity to ascertain the likelihood of whether or not they were getting involved with a twat. The second call, a mere two days later, was made by Lisa from work. Quite spontaneous of her I have to say—either she was incredibly bored and had me on speakerphone for the amusement of her work colleagues or, and more likely I would like to think, she was satisfied that I posed no immediate threat to her personal safety and sanity and decided to give it a lash.

    I am generally free to talk during what people call the 'working day', and we had a good twenty-minute chat about different stuff. None of it earth shattering I have to say, but it was a pleasant diversion, nonetheless, and reassured me that were we to actually meet for a drink or dinner, polite conversation would not be lacking. A week or so of chat followed before I cut to the chase and asked her if she wanted to get a bite to eat. Thankfully, she quickly and graciously acquiesced and arrangements for the rendezvous were made.

if nothing else, a date with Lisa would be good practice for me as I limbered up for the main event—my assignation with Daisy, which if there was a God, was bound to happen in a matter of time.

And so 7.00pm on the appointed day found me recumbent in a leather club chair enjoying a glass of wine in the salubrious bar of The Fitzwilliam Hotel. Not the most atmospheric location, agreed, but I chose it for tactical reasons over those of a romantic nature. I was familiar with the place you see, having had a couple of informal meetings there over the course of the previous months. Knowing the layout of a place where one intends to meet a person for the first time is quite important, I think: you just feel more comfortable strolling in to somewhere you've been to before. (If, for chivalrous reasons you give the other party free reign to choose the venue and it is somewhere not known to you, I would suggest that, at the very least, you go for a 'reconnaissance' drink there before the night of your meeting.) So, though this particular bar might have been somewhat lacking in ambience, I felt it was ideal for our purposes. It wasn't too big, it wasn't too dark and it wasn't too noisy. Key requirements I think you'll agree, for a meeting such as this. Also, there was a good amount of space between the tables so you could chat away without having some nosy sod next door earwigging on your delicate opening exchanges, the way I would myself.

Anyway, as I said, there I was, enjoying my wine, relaxing in my comfy chair—which afforded me an unimpeded view of the single door into the bar from the hotel lobby—waiting for Lisa to arrive. We had agreed on 7.30 but I naturally got there at 7.00 to secure my seat of choice and have a drink before she arrived. I had of course, previously asked her what she looked like—just so I'd recognise her I had said—and she answered, rather enigmatically I thought, 'I'm tallish, tall for a girl anyway, I suppose, with long black straight hair. That's all I'm telling you. I don't want to give too much away!', so I was keeping an eye out for ladies of such a description.

Finally, at 7.48pm, half-way through my second glass of wine, Lisa decided to join me and strolled in, cool as you like, not in the slightest bit bothered about being twenty minutes late. Ten minutes would have been fair enough, but twenty was stretching it, I thought.

I stood to greet her as she approached. And also to check her out properly, of course. I have to say, my first impressions were not that favourable. Though she was fairly good looking, and appeared pleasant enough, I just didn't feel there was going to be a connection of any kind between us. That might sound ridiculous in light of the fact that we hadn't actually spoken to each other face to face yet, but that's where I was coming from as she strolled towards me, overly ecstatic smile on her face like someone had a gun to her back.

'Lisa, hi. Donal. How are you?'

'Donal, hi, hi. I'm fine thanks. And you? You here long?'

'No, not really. Ten minutes or so.'

'Oh good, good. I couldn't get a taxi,' she said.

'Long walk.'

'Sorry? Oh right. Very funny. I got one *event*ually,' she said.

'Fair enough. Would you like a drink?'

'Ahm, let me see now . . . I think, I'll have, a . . .'

No rush.

'. . . Ahm, yeah. I'll have a mineral water, please. Sparkling.'

God Almighty. Twenty minutes to decide to what she's going to drink and she opts for a mineral water. Hate to see her on a sixty-second quiz.

'No problem. Be right back,' I said, getting up and turning towards the bar. There were two very deferential Asian chaps lolling around, dying for something to do, but only a minute into the proceedings, I needed a reprieve. This was not going well. What was wrong with me? Why couldn't I get over myself and give things a chance to pan out? What's the worst that could happen? Two or three hours of this kind of torment, that's what, I thought. Okay, she was 'nice'.[2] Big deal. Nice ain't enough. I don't want nice.

2. For my money, 'nice' is one of the most offensive words in the English language. If given one word to sum me up and somebody said I was 'nice' I'd be disgusted, because, to my mind, it means I had no impact on them, either positively or negatively. I'd much rather they'd say I was a cynic, because at least it's specific. At least it means they were paying attention to me, and made a judgment based on what they discerned. 'Nice' doesn't cover any ground in my book. So when I refer to Lisa as being 'nice', I am using the word in a near-pejorative context, much the same as most people do, however unwittingly.

The barman approached and asked me what I wanted. Okay, I was in a public bar, standing at the counter with money in my hand—it was hardly a surreal moment, but it did give me pause for thought. What *do* I want? I want fucking extraordinary,[3] that's what I want, I answered definitively.

'Mineral water please. Sparkling.'

'Now, there you go,' I said, placing the drink down on the table.

'Great, thanks a million,' Lisa said graciously, taking a generous sip from the glass before setting it down on the table, wiping a stray rivulet of Ballygowan from her lip as she did so. Which could have been a very sexy gesture, intended or not, in the right context. That context being my finding her irresistibly attractive. Which I didn't, so she just looked like a slobbering eight-year-old who had gulped down too much Coke.

'No problem. So what's the plan? You hungry?' I asked, trying to keep on track.

'Yeah, I'm starving actually. Been on the go all day today—work's a bit manic at the minute—didn't have time for lunch,' Lisa answered enthusiastically.

'Oh yeah? What area are you in?' I enquired politely.

'Servers,' she said emphatically, like it was a matter of national security.

'Right. And do you like it?'

'Love it. It's a very competitive segment.'

3. Apologies for the rather coarse language, but they were extenuating circumstances. You see, a couple of years ago I decided that, above all, I wanted my life to be extraordinary. Not in the sense that I would feel perpetually unfulfilled if I didn't spend a couple of weeks living with the Secoya people deep in Ecuador's Oriente province learning their customs. (Not that I wouldn't do that—I just wouldn't do it to say I'd done it. If I decide I really want to do it, then I will. But I don't. Not yet anyway.) I mean extraordinary in the literal sense of the word. Without getting all etymological on you, 'extra' is Latin for 'outside of', and ordinary is, well, you know—plain, dull, banal, uninspiring, take your pick. I've no fixed definition of what it is I do actually want, in general life terms, never mind in terms of a potential soulmate; all I know is I want them both to be extraordinary. Conversely, 'ordinary' is of no interest to me at all.

I hate the way people use that word 'segment' when talking about their job. An orange has segments, a career doesn't.

'So you like to be under a bit of pressure then?'

'Yeah, I suppose I do. Brings out the best in me, I think,' she said, doing her best to flash me a flirtatious grin, which I decided to write off as her being a little nervous. 'And what about you? You must be under a lot of pressure being a writer, no? Deadlines and all that.'

'Not really, to be honest. Not in the same way as most people would be in a regular job with sales or performance targets and what not. With me, I'm given a delivery date that's normally six or nine months away, so if I applied myself properly there'd be no pressure. Of course, I don't apply myself properly at all. I spend months thinking about whatever it is I'm supposed to be working on—how I'm going to do it, what structure it'll take, what research I need to do, *where* I'm going to do it even. Anything to avoid actually doing it. And then I nearly kill myself lashing into it in the last few months. But at least it's self-inflicted pressure.'

'And do you not find it lonely? Working away on your own all the time? I know I wouldn't like it.'

'No, not particularly. I'm not much of a team player to be honest. Unless I'm the team leader. And even then, I'd be conscious of the possibility that my team members mightn't be up to it, so I'd nearly rather do everything myself anyway.'

'Well, that's the whole point about being a team leader when you think about it. Analysing everyone's strengths and weaknesses and drawing the best you can from each person to achieve whatever the objective is,' Lisa said, as if quoting from some redundant textbook.

'Yeah, yeah, I know. That's the theory, but it doesn't normally work out that way. There'll always be some moron who'll drag you down. I remember first year in college we got a project to do—had to pick a company on the stock exchange and analyse it from every angle. At first I thought it was an individual thing. Then the lecturer, who was a complete moron, tells us that we have to do it in teams of four. I had missed a couple of lectures and by the time I heard this, the only remaining 'team members' available to me were these three gobshites who hadn't a clue. Ended up doing the whole thing myself.'

'God, you're definitely not a team player, are you? I'd hate to have to work with you!' Lisa said jokingly. At least that's the way I took it.

'Anyway, that's enough about that. Food. How about the Market Bar?' I ventured casually, when in fact this was the only place I had any intention of going to: the food was good, the service was quick, and it was very casual. Cheap too, which was a valid consideration as I'd no doubt be springing for the evening's entertainment.

'Sounds great, I haven't actually been there yet but I've heard it's really good.'

So far, so boring. But wait for this: fifteen minutes later we're in the Market Bar, seated at one of the long tables, deciding on what to have. I'd decided before we got there: spicy meatballs. Lisa had to go through practically every item on the menu—out loud— and weigh up its pros and cons. Fair enough, it was her first time there, but it's not like the food on offer was a million miles from what you'd get in lots of other places. Finally plumping for the chicken brochettes (bad call—there's not enough of them), she again opted for mineral water when the cute little Spanish waitress asked us what we'd like to drink.

'Nothing to drink, no? Are you one of these not-on-a-school-night- disciplinarians then?' I probed.

'No, it's not that. Well actually, I wouldn't really drink that much during the week normally, but I'm not supposed to drink right now, if you know what I mean,' she replied somewhat coyly.

'No, I don't. What do you mean? Are you pregnant?' I said laughing.

'Yes, I am.'

'What? You're pregnant?' I kind of shouted, much to the bemusement of the two women dining at the other end of our table who proceeded to exchange furtive, knowing glances.

'Yes. Is that a problem?' Lisa enquired calmly.

'Ah, kinda. Why didn't you tell me?' I protested.

'Because I didn't want you to judge me before you'd met me, that's why,' Lisa said quite reasonably, however annoyingly.

'Jesus, this is unbelievable. Of all the ads I could have answered, I pick you and you're pregnant, of all things,' I continued.

'"Of all things",' Lisa said in a slightly hurt tone. 'What's that supposed to mean?'

Realising how ignorant my previous comment had been—I really should learn to distinguish between when to actually say something and when to just think it to myself—I looked at her and smiled weakly. 'Sorry, that's wasn't cool. It's just ironic that you're pregnant, as opposed to say, being, I don't know, a Mormon or a recovering alcoholic or something. Kids aren't my thing at all, I have to say.'

'Well I didn't think they were necessarily my thing either, not at this point anyway—I'd always planned to have them, just a little later on when I was more settled—but I just found out I was pregnant a little while ago and I've decided to accept it, sorry wrong word, embrace it, and move on.'

'Fair play. You're dead right, I admire that,' I said, meaning it, too, 'it's just that I find it quite strange that you're on a blind date, having dinner here with me, and you're, like, pregnant, that's all.'

'I'm eating for two now,' Lisa said chirpily as our food arrived. 'I think what you're trying to say is that you find it strange that I'm here having dinner with you and not the father of my child?' she continued perceptively when the waitress left, saving me the grief of trying to tactfully ask that very question.

'Yeah. It does seem a little odd. Fair enough, it's none of my business, so don't tell me anything you don't want to, but anything you do tell me will have to wait a minute because I need a cigarette,' I said, rising from the table and grabbing my smokes from my jacket pocket.

'You smoke?' Lisa said disgustedly. 'Why didn't you tell me?'

'*Touché*,' I said smiling. 'I guess I didn't want you to judge me before you'd met me.'

Enjoying my smoke outside I thought about Lisa's revelation. It was a gutsy thing to do and no doubt. Having a child within a stable relationship isn't easy—which is another reason why I don't want one—but going it alone and raising one on your own is really asking for it. Fair play to her. It's an extraordinary thing she's doing all right, but it's the wrong kind of extraordinary for me, I thought as I stubbed out my cigarette.

'How's the chicken?' I asked as I sat back down.

'It's good, actually. Not enough of it, though, I should have gone for the large one,' Lisa answered.

'Told you,' I said pettily as I tucked into my meatballs. 'So. Tell me what you want to tell me.'

'Do you want the headlines or all the details?' Lisa asked thoughtfully.

'Headlines first,' I said, 'I'll be asking plenty of questions, don't worry.'

'Well, basically,' Lisa started, putting down her knife and fork, 'I was going out with a guy for four years, everything going fairly well, ups and downs, but that's the way it goes. We bought a house last year. Moved in, got a lawnmower, blah, blah blah. Then three months ago we went to Prague for a weekend and a couple of weeks later I missed my period. I bought a kit and did the test and it came up positive. I didn't say anything to Barry at the time because I wanted to be sure first, so I went to the doctor and . . .'

'No medical bits if you don't mind, I'm eating,' I interjected.

'Don't be such an idiot,' she returned. 'So I went to the doctor and he confirmed it for me. That was a Thursday, so I waited until the next day to tell Barry when he came home from work—he's a rep and he's always down the country during the week—and he . . . just . . . lost it. Completely lost it. Said it couldn't be his, that he always used protection and all that kind of thing, like it was a disease or something. So, huge big screaming row, I did the usual and went back to my mum's for the weekend, he did the usual and went off and got pissed with all his rugger mates and didn't even call me. So that's that. It's just baby and me from here on.'

'Wow, that's fairly mad all right,' I surmised as Lisa returned to her food. 'But surely you must have talked about it again when you'd both calmed down?'

'Oh, yeah, we did. Loads. He apologised for everything he'd said, and obviously accepted that the child was his, but he was adamant that he didn't want to get married and that there was no point in staying together for the sake of the baby. Once I heard that and knew he was being honest, I despised him and didn't want anything more to do with him. I'd rather be on my own than with a spineless shit like that.'

'Too right. He sounds like a complete tosser. What's his name? Barry?'

'Yeah.'

'And where's Barry from?'

'Castleknock.'

'And what kind of repping does Barry do?'

'He works for his dad.

'God. Castleknock. Rugger bugger. Works for daddy. How could you have been so blind?' I said mockingly.

'I know, I know,' Lisa laughed, covering her mouth with her hand. 'He's a bit younger than me and I suppose he still thinks he's . . .'

'What age is he?'

'27.'

'And what age are you again?'

'God. I'm 30, if you must know.'

'Really? You look older.'

Shit. Did it again.

'Jesus, thanks very much. You're a great confidence booster.'

'No, in a good way like. You look like a real woman I mean, not like a girl . . .'

'So I'm fat as well?'

'What? I never said you were *fat*. You're not fat at all. You will be in a few months' time, and quite possibly for some time after that, but . . .' I said trying to make light of my apparent gaffe.

'Piss off,' she parried, rising to the bait playfully.

Food finished, Lisa justified having a slice of cheesecake on both the inadequacy of her main portion and the fact that she was, 'with child and could do whatever the hell' she wanted. I had another glass of wine and we chatted away happily, each much more comfortable than we were an hour and a half before.

Obviously, Lisa gathered from my reaction to her news that I wasn't potential husband material. That I wasn't even worth considering going out with probably, and had decided to just enjoy the evening for what it was worth and let a stranger ask her loads of questions and buy her dinner. And that was just dandy with me. I liked her a lot more then than I did when I first met her. When she walked into the bar of the hotel and took about twenty minutes to decide she was going to have a mineral water, I didn't really like her, which was both grossly unfair and incredibly stupid of me. But there you go, that's the way it is. (Well actually, 'like' is probably the wrong word to use there. I didn't fancy her when I first met her. I still didn't fancy her an hour or so later, especially after learning of her impending arrival, but I did like her, and I did admire her.)

We finished up about half an hour later and decided to call it a night. After gladly paying the very reasonable bill, I walked Lisa outside to George's Street and showed her how to find a taxi. She went home to her house on her own, full of both the potential joys and trepidations of single parenthood, and I went home to my house on my own, glad I had met her.

———

'Preggers? How do we feel about that?' Paul asked when I rang him the following day.

'Not great, obviously. Told her straight out too. We got on grand, though, she's a lovely girl, you know? Good fun, doesn't take herself too seriously or anything.'

'Any action?'

'She's pregnant, you fool. With child: she's hardly gonna be up for a tumble in her condition.'

'You never know. Hormones racing—she could be a bit gamey. Rach was all over the place. Maybe we should hang in there for a bit?'

'Said we'll keep in touch and all, but that's about it.'

'Fair enough so. Who's up next?' he asked.

'Think I'll have a crack at that nurse, Elaine, when I get back from my holidays.'

'That's more like it. At least we know nurses are game for a laugh. Any word from your one in *Vogue*?'

'No, not yet. She must be away. Should hear something soon though.'

'Yeah, hopefully. Punching above our weight there—be cool to get something going with her. Listen, I have to go—the little fella needs changing. Enjoy France. How long you away for?'

'Only a week. I will. Good luck.'

09

I tell you something, when you're hot, you're hot. Not only was the lovely Vera in Ryazan ready to pack her bags and fly in an westerly direction to marry me, but when I got back from France and checked my e-mails, what was waiting for me only a reply from none other than Ms Daisy Garnett![1] Result or what? For your delectation, I hereby reproduce the text of said electronic message:

Dear Donal,
Thanks a million for that delicious bottle of Bushmills. Sorry for not replying sooner but I have been away. I'm a huge Bushmills fan. And what a lovely package to open up on a Monday morning . . . and such a nice letter. I don't know what to say . . . I'm sort of between everything at the moment . . . but am around in London, so if you are over here anyway of course let's go for a drink, but only when you're next in town. Meanwhile, what sort of writing do you do full time? I find it such an odd thing to do—such a gift and yet such a bore . . . and of course I'm on deadine so

1. I spent an idyllic week tucked away in a small cabin nestled in a pine forest in the Landes region of France. As I said, it was idyllic but I was miles from an internet connection and so couldn't check my e-mails.

must get back and put my nose to grindstone . . . would love to get on my bicycle, lie in the park and drink some of that whiskey . . . but another time . . .

But thank you—what a thoughtful, generous thing to do for anyone, never mind a stranger.

Daisy

Naturally, a pivotal piece of correspondence such as this merited close scrutiny and detailed analysis. And so, after reading it sixteen times over the course of an hour, progressively mining its seams ever deeper as I did so, I came to the fundamentally sound conclusion that I had made quite an impact on the delectable Ms Garnett.[2] I mean, look at the evidence:

1) '**Dear** *Donal*'
Not a formal, 'Hello Donal', or simply, 'Donal', or the more casual, 'Hi Donal'. No. Not a bit of it. Daisy opted for the much more sincere and intimate '***Dear*** Donal'.

2) '*Thanks **a million** . . .*'
Not, 'Thank you so much', or, 'Thank you very much', or anything as boring as that. Oh, no, because neither of them would have adequately conveyed the sheer depth of gratitude which Daisy wanted to convey to me for the wondrous gift. Which is why she went for, '*Thanks **a million**'.

3) '*I'm a huge **Bushmills** fan.*'
An overt acknowledgement of her admiration for the premium Irish whiskey, despite her *Vogue* bio suggesting that Scotch was her drink of her choice? And she's half-Irish? Think about it.

4) '*. . . and such **a nice letter**.*'
The contents and witty phraseology of the accompanying letter were obviously to her pleasing; which is only right after the amount of effort I put into it.[3]

2. My own conclusion met with Paul's considered opinion, who declared us set for 'an away game' in the very near future.

5) '*I don't know what to* **say** *...*'

The '...' are hugely significant here, I think you'll agree. Once again, so overcome was she with sheer joy at the receipt of my package that Daisy had to restrain herself in her expression of gratitude. She wanted to say so much more. Probably had, in fact, but later revised the e-mail before sending it and decided to hold back a little. For now.

6) '***I'm sort of between everything at the moment...***'

A momentous sentence, if ever there was one. Loaded with possibility, too. And the '...' at the end is basically the equivalent of Daisy having highlighted the whole sentence in bold type, the way I have just now, so eager was she to ensure that I pay it due attention and read into it what she in her heart wanted to say. In essence, what she was trying to convey to me here was that I should not pay too much heed to the closing paragraph of her *Vogue* article, where she remarked that she had been on a few dates with some guy she used to know in New York years back. 'I'm in a bit of a tizz at the minute, and you have just turned my whole world upside down. Please believe me when I say that there is very little of substance to the relationship,' she was effectively saying. And I heard her.

7) '*... of course let's go for* **a** *drink ...*'

A blind man could see what the angle here was. *A* drink, indeed! Very coy, Ms Garnett. Very coy.

I rest my case.

---

3. Admittedly, it would have been more pleasing to me had 'beautiful' or 'gorgeous' or 'magnificent' been substituted for 'nice'. However, after due consideration, I would humbly suggest that one or other of the above alternatives may well have been called upon in the first instance, only to be later replaced with 'nice', so apprehensive was Daisy about revealing the extent of her true feelings at this early stage.

A couple of days later I had to scoot into town to attend my psychiatrist, Dr Fielding.[4] By way of illustrating to her just how unnecessary, and quite frankly rather tiring, these meetings had become in light of the progress I was making on the benefit-of-the-doubt front, indeed, on all fronts, I decided to bring along with me a copy of Daisy's joyous message and my list of incisive observations thereon, as annotated above. During the previous couple of chats with Dr Fielding, I got the distinct impression that she didn't really consider my participation in the dating game to be sufficiently remedial in nature, and that were more 'fundamental issues' to be addressed. Well, today I'd show her.

A rather attractive temporary secretary—whose name I soon learnt was Yvonne—greeted me in reception, and politely informed me that Dr Fielding was just on her way back from lunch and would be with me in a matter of minutes. I sat down and picked up a magazine, pretending to be engrossed in its contents. I was of course, not reading the magazine at all—I was gazing longingly at Yvonne across the room from me. Rather attractive

4. Not so much *my* psychiatrist really; just *a* psychiatrist whom I happen to have been attending once a month for the last while. No idea why, really, it's not like there's anything wrong with me, but my local GP (from whom I sought assistance with my sleeping disorder), last year somehow diagnosed me as being borderline delusional—I know, the sheer lunacy of it all!—and referred me to this Dr Fielding in order to ascertain the extent of the 'problem'. Clearly, the poor chap was off his trolley and could have done worse than see a shrink himself, but he was an old friend of my uncle's and I didn't want to embarrass him, so I played along with him and went to see Dr Fielding as suggested.

Dr Fielding turned out to be a woman too, if you don't mind. And not only was Dr Fielding a woman, but she was a very elegant woman to boot, and I enjoyed the *frisson* that enveloped our discussions as she probed my expansive mind, searching for clues as to the nature of my nature, as it were. (Sadly, she was a little old for my liking. Married too, I surmised from the few occasions when I managed to swing our little *tête-à-têtes* around and do a little probing of my own.) Also in her favour was the location of her consulting rooms: next to a lively bar, to which I could adjourn after our meetings, or 'sessions' as she liked to call them.

didn't cover it at all—she was actually gorgeous: slender yet full bodied, with long, thick, rich hair, the colour of Belgian chocolate. Quite something to behold on a not-so-sunny summer afternoon. Where did they live, these delightful creatures? I never seemed to be in the same orbit as them whenever I was out. Maybe it was my not having a job? After all, if I was gainfully employed I would have reason to leave the house every morning at a set time to go to work, and I would be out for lunch—just like Dr Fielding was— every day, exposing myself, if you will, to any number of lovelies like Yvonne that no doubt populated the working world.

My reverie was cut short by the arrival of the good doctor, who apologised profusely for being late and ushered me graciously in to her inner sanctum. Just as well too, really—my lustful thoughts about Yvonne were tantamount to infidelity, and that wouldn't be fair on Daisy, seeing as how we'd only just met. (Well, not met exactly, but you know what I mean.)

I took up my usual position on the leather recliner and waited for Dr Fielding to kick off. She took a slim folder from a large steel filing cabinet and sat on the sofa opposite me, where she flicked through some notes from our last meeting, nodding silently as she reacquainted herself with me and my alleged neuroses. Satisfied she had a handle on who I was again, she looked at me and smiled benignly.

'So, Donal, when we last spoke, you were telling me about the various methods you were employing in your attempts to improve the quality of your personal life. What progress, if any, have you to report on the success of this approach?'

'If I may borrow a phrase you use yourself quite regularly, Doctor, I'd say that "real and substantial" progress has been made on a number of fronts,' I said determinedly, knowing what response it would bring.

'Really?' she answered, no little amount of suspicion in her voice. 'Would you care to elaborate on that for me, please?'

'Certainly. As you know, I joined a couple of dating websites, and through these I have come into contact with a few different women, mostly in the UK, so admittedly the logistics aren't that great, but the communication end of things itself is going fine.

However, up until a couple of weeks ago, I would have to say that in all honesty, none of them made the earth move for me, if you know what I mean. They're probably all perfectly nice in their own way and all; it's just that I didn't feel there was that much common ground on which to try and build something, you know?'

'Until a couple of weeks ago, you said. What happened then?' Dr Fielding then asked, her curiosity roused.

'Quite a lot, actually. I was reading this article in *Vogue* that a friend of mine had given me. And it was written by this woman called Daisy Garnett, who recounted her own story of how she had fared when she tried the whole online-dating thing, you see? Great article it was too, very insightful. So anyway, as I was reading the article I found myself becoming very attracted to the narrator, and when I finished reading, there on the contributors' page was a photo of Daisy—she's gorgeous, by the way; short blonde hair, very uncooperative, has to wear a clip, blue eyes, lovely skin, beautiful features, the real deal—and a few personal details. Kind of a mini cv, I suppose. Totally amazing woman. She's sailed across the Atlantic Ocean, ridden a camel across the Syrian desert, lived in New York for eight years, loves needlepoint, her sisters, Scotch whiskey . . . kinda messy in appearance, that shabby-chic thing I suppose you'd call it . . . What else? Oh, yeah, she's half-Irish too. Anyway, that's Daisy; like I said she's totally amazing. So, I'm thinking about her and decide that she's just the type of woman I'd like to go out with, you know? Cool, and adventurous. Warm and outgoing. Beautiful. Everything I'm not, ha ha, so I . . .'

'And how do you know she's not already happily involved with somebody?' the doctor interrupted.

'Because at the end of the article she said that she had kind of met someone, some guy she used to half know when she lived in New York as it turned out, but that it was early days and they'd only been on a couple of dates. So, she's fair game. No ring.'

'I see,' replied Dr Fielding, barely suppressing a rueful tone. 'And what do you propose to do about your attraction to this Ms Garnett?'

'Ah. Not do, but done: I sent her a letter. Not a love letter, now, or anything like that, give me some credit. It was just a general kind of letter—quite brilliantly written though, if I may say so—

saying "hi" and what have you, telling her I had read the article and thought it was great, and that she was great, and a little bit about me and where I'm at. That kind of thing. And then I finished up by saying that if and when her little dalliance with the guy from NYC came to nothing, I'd like to buy her dinner.'

'Really?' said Dr Fielding, a little taken aback, I thought.

'Really,' I replied confidently.

'And what exactly do you hope to achieve with this letter, might I ask?'

'Wrong again, Doctor. It's not a question of what I hope to achieve, but what I have achieved, for this very morning I received a rather wonderful e-mail from Ms Garnett, thanking me most profusely for my gift and letter. She . . .'

'Gift? You sent her a gift with the letter?' she then asked inquisitively.

'Oh yeah, I forgot to tell you. Well, Daisy likes Scotch, you see? And she's half-Irish, right? She said so in her little mini cv thing on the contributors' page. And she wouldn't have said it if it wasn't something she was proud of, or thought was cool. And I'm a hundred per cent Irish, yeah? But obviously I wasn't going to come straight out and say that in the letter—look like a bit of a twat, as if that was all I had going for me or something! But I wanted to work it in somehow all the same, so I sent her a bottle of Irish whiskey. You see? Clever, no? And not just any old whiskey. Bushmills 16-year-old whiskey. Serious stuff. Went down a storm with her.'

'I'm glad to hear it,' said Dr Fielding, sitting forward earnestly on the edge of the sofa. 'It sounds like a very thoughtful gift. But what do you think is going to happen from here on? Did Ms Garnett give any indication of how she might see things proceeding, if there is to be any proceeding, or did she seem to think that this was a one-off communication and that . . .'

'One-off? I don't think so,' I interjected rather tersely. 'She was utterly charming. I took the liberty of bringing a copy of the e-mail with me to show you. Would you like to read it?'

'Very much so, if I may.'

'Absolutely. And, I did that exercise with it. You know the one you showed me before when I got those rejection letters from those publishers in the UK who said they wouldn't take my next book, and I was really pissed off about it? And you worked through the letter with me, analysing each sentence and the language used to extract the positives from it?'

'Yes, yes, I know the exercise you're referring to,' said Dr Fielding, getting up from the sofa to read the printout I was holding aloft like an Olympic medal. A gold Olympic medal.

She read the e-mail quickly while standing there beside me, and then raising her glasses to rub her eyes, sighed gently and said to me, 'It's a very nice message to receive, no doubt, but it is . . . rather innocuous, don't you think?'

'Innocuous?' I snorted derisorily. 'I don't think so. Like you said, read between the lines, examine the language. Look for the positives. That's all I did.'

'And do you have your list of "positives" with you as well?' she then enquired.

'Yes, I do. Would you like to see them?'

'Yes, indeed I would.'

I unfurled myself from the recliner and produced the two pages of observations I had made on Daisy's message. Dr Fielding scanned them quickly and then took a deep breath.

'Very comprehensive. Tell you what, Donal. How about I look at this in some detail and then try the exercise for myself. From the standpoint of a neutral observer. And then we can compare your list of observations with mine, and see what we can learn from that. Okay?'

'Sure thing, yeah. Tell you what though, you could just photocopy my list and you'd be done!' I suggested rather cleverly. Lord, I can be arch!

Dr Fielding didn't seem to take my witticism in the manner it was intended however, and retreated to her desk with the paperwork, where she sat in silence with her notepad.

'Okay if I pop out for a quick smoke while you do that?' I asked.

'Of course, if you must,' she answered quietly, not deigning to look at me while she spoke.

A tad gloomy at her apparent lack of enthusiasm for my efforts, I took my leave and exited the room. What a rollercoaster life is!

As I entered the reception area again, my spirits soared at the sight of the delectable Yvonne reaching up on her tippy-toes to retrieve a box file from a high shelf, her sheer white linen shirt riding high above the waistband of her tight-fitting black trousers revealing a delicious slice of brown belly to my greedy eyes. 'Oh, to kiss that belly! To press my face against it like a beggar.'[5]

'Can I help you with that at all?' I said politely.

'No, no. It's fine thanks, I have it,' she said cheerfully, hauling the box from the shelf and moving gracefully towards her desk.

'Indeed you do,' I ventured somewhat cheekily. And most uncharacteristically I must say—didn't know what was coming over me, but I felt a surge of confidence well up within me. Must have been the effect of Daisy's letter. Yvonne smiled demurely at me and resumed her work.

'Just popping out for a smoke. Be back in a few minutes.'

'No problem, Donal,' she said breezily.

Donal. She used my name, I reflected as I leaned against the exterior wall of the building, inhaling my cigarette and the sights of the city around me. How familiar! God, she was a live one, wasn't she? And what a belly! I could spend a week nestled in there. And Lord knows I could do with the break. Stop it, man! You have Daisy now, what are you thinking? No, it's okay—I have the exclusivity rule on my side. Smitten as I am with Ms Garnett, and much as I'm sure she is with me, or at least will be when things progress, I am essentially a free agent. And given the dearth of physical interaction with females recently, aligning myself totally to one woman, especially to one I haven't actually met, would not be the wisest course of action. No, free as a bird, me. What to do re Yvonne though? I could hardly ask her out, could I? Well, I suppose I could, and she might say yes, too, if her flirtatious behaviour today was anything to go by. Fielding wouldn't approve, I'm sure, might try to scupper things between us. Give her a look at my file, maybe. Would she? Could she? I'd have her disbarred! It's all rubbish as well: 'borderline delusional' indeed. First off, I would have thought that borders didn't come into it—one is either delusional or one is not. And secondly, I clearly was not

5. That man Ames again. You really should seek him out.

delusional. Possessed of an active imagination and creative mind, yes. Both essential characteristics for somebody in my line of work. But delusional, no. Not me. Fielding maybe! Ha!

'All done?' I enquired breezily as I retook my position on the recliner.

'Yes, all done. And my observations would appear to be quite at variance with your own very thorough analysis of Ms Garnett's e-mail.'

'Really? How so?' I asked perplexedly.

'Well, Donal, the purpose of the exercise is to examine a particular communication on a rational level, without getting emotive about the contents. And I don't think that's what you've done in this instance,' Dr Fielding said to my considerable surprise, moving to the sofa once again to continue her assault on me. 'On the basis of reading an article in *Vogue* magazine written by this woman, the contents of which may or may not even be true—all writers avail of poetic licence from time to time, as you yourself can attest to—you decided that you were attracted to Ms Garnett. Perhaps on a whim, perhaps not, you sent her a letter and gift, and waited expectantly for her to get in touch with you. She sent you an e-mail this morning to thank you for the gift and letter, which was only proper—it was a thoughtful thing to do. But I don't really believe there is enough in the content of this e-mail to suggest that Ms Garnett feels the way about you as you evidently seem to feel about her . . .'

'Are we talking about the same e-mail here?' I blurted, utterly exasperated at the direction her comments were going.

'Please let me finish. And why should she feel anything towards you, other than a passing sense of gratitude for a generous gift received? She's never met you. She doesn't know the first thing about you. I think you read the message, and took it to mean what you *wanted* it to mean, not what it actually means, thereby deluding yourself into thinking that yourself and Ms Garnett have a romantic future together. And I don't believe . . .'

This was going too far, it really was. I rose from the recliner and took a deep breath.

'Deluded? I am not deluded, Dr Fielding. I am attracted to Ms Garnett, to Daisy, and whilst I agree that she has not as yet professed her undying love for me, I think it perfectly reasonable to infer from her correspondence that she did not find me to be a reprehensible character and would be amenable to going for a drink or dinner with me when I am next in London. That would be any sane person's reading of that e-mail.'

'Possibly. But then again, maybe what Ms Garnett was really trying to say in her message was that she appreciated the gift and that was that. The bit about going for a drink could well have been somewhat . . . playful on her part, would you not think?'

'No I would not think,' I said testily. 'And if you'll excuse me, I have to go now. Goodbye.'

And with that I left the office, barely managing to summon the energy to smile at Yvonne as I left, whose body language intimated to me that she would have been open to a little chit-chat. And so now her day was ruined as well! All because of bloody Fielding and her negative vibes. I decided to repair to the bar next door and have a much needed drink before going home to prepare my follow-up to Daisy's reply, which itself was another crucial piece of correspondence: too much too soon and I might ward her off; too little too late and she might think I'd lost interest.

Things were certainly picking up now, though. Just as well I was off on hols again soon—all this activity was beginning to feel like work.

10

B y the end of June I had a number of ladies to commune with on one level or another—Jane, Rebecca, Vera and Natalya,[1] not to mention the trio of vixens 'winking' suggestively at me on the Anotherfriend website.

1. Natalya, a 26-year-old student, sought me out on the Dating Direct site recently. Like Vera, Natalya lived in Russia, in a place called Pskov, south-southwest of St Petersburg, in the north-western region of the country, near the Estonian border.

Dating from the eighth century, Pskov, a city with a population of some 200,000 people, is an important rail junction in the heart of a flax-growing area. Industries include food processing and the manufacture of metals, machinery, building materials, and linen. Known in antiquity as Pleskov, its large-scale stone construction shows that it was already a rich town in the 12th century. In 1347 Pskov became an independent, democratic city-state and a flourishing commercial centre. It was the capital of the Pskov Republic from 1348 to 1510, at which point it was annexed by Moscow, thereby losing its democratic institutions. Its importance, except as a strategic fortress, soon declined. In 1917 the railroad station at Pskov was the scene of the abdication of Nicholas II. The historic core of Pskov is the inner walled city, which contains a kremlin with towers in the Byzantine style, a cathedral, and numerous medieval churches and monasteries. (I was brushing up on my history and geography, seeing as how I was such a hit with the ladies from these parts.)

Natalya's opening gambit went like this:

In the inbox I found a couple of e-mails of some note. The first was from Dr Fielding apologising for any upset she had caused me with her frank tone the other day. And proper order too—I hope she apologised to Yvonne as well for ruining what could have been a delightful end to her day. She added that she had taken the liberty of attaching a copy of her list of observations about Daisy's e-mail, seeing as how we didn't actually get around to discussing them, and expressed her hope that I would have a chance to look over it before our next meeting. I sent a firm but polite reply, stating that I accepted her apology but felt that our time together was no longer of any discernible benefit to me and that I would in fact, not be returning to see her at any point in the foreseeable future. I thanked her for her efforts thus far but noted that we seemed to be at cross purposes as to what constituted 'delusional' behaviour and finished by saying that I felt perfectly comfortable proceeding as I saw fit. Message sent, and chapter closed, as it were. I didn't even bother opening the attachment.

The second e-mail of note was from Vera in Ryazan. Things between us were certainly moving on apace as far she was concerned—I might have to refer her to Dr Fielding if this kept up. Guess what her e-mail said?

1. *contd*

   Hello!!!

   My name is Natalya. To me 24 years. I have seen your structure, and it has very much interested me. I think that I with you can correspond. How do you think? I think that you are the interesting person and we can learn about each other more. If I have interested you, you can write to me on my electronic address: —
   ——————@gawab.com, or with your letter.

   With the best regards,
   Natalya

Charming as the lady appeared to be, I figured she was, like Vera, another bunny-boiler dying to get out of Russia and head West for the good life. Flattered, I sent a polite message back to her, only to receive two days later, another missive along the lines of what Vera had written previously, imploring me to 'become one' with her and 'make the strong family' etc. And another, even more beseeching exhortation followed a couple of days after that. I had to nip it in the bud, so I blocked her from sending me any further messages, much to Paul's disappointment.

Well, you will pay my arrival to you and all documents necessary for it?
Your Vera

That's it. In its entirety. No hello, no nothing. I was stupefied. Had I missed out on the dozen or so e-mails and phone calls which might conceivably have given her good reason to feel that our 'relationship' had blossomed to this point? What was it about my last rather terse e-mail that she didn't understand? I know I'm worth chasing and all that, but enough's enough—time to cut her off once and for all. I decided that the best course of action was to take no action and just ignore her and hope that my silence would convey to her what my hopelessly inadequate command of the English language had failed to do.

Next was an e-mail from the organisers of a speed-dating-type do happening the following month that I had registered for, confirming receipt of my payment and expressing their delight at my willingness to subject myself to the humiliation of participating in such an event.

Rebecca, my society heiress in Belgravia, had also sent me another little instalment on how life was treating her. As with her previous communiqués, the content was less than riveting but she a very pleasant and well-meaning woman, if a sandwich or two short of a full picnic in terms of the depth of her discourse. Still and all, I liked her well enough and thought it best to hang in there for the crack—hopefully when I went to London to visit Daisy I could 'double down' and work Rebecca into the schedule as well.

I also joined yet another dating website. This one went by the entirely functional name of Dating in Ireland, and though the graphics were a little dull, it was by far the most comprehensive one I'd come across on my travels. The amount of information I was requested to supply was unreal. Apart from where you described why someone should get to know you and who constituted your ideal match, all the answers to every other question could be selected from a range of options supplied in a drop-down menu, so it didn't actually take that long to fill in. Check out what I ended up with:

Narky

About Him

Country of Origin:	Ireland
Current Location:	Dublin, Ireland
Gender:	Male
Age:	35
Star Sign:	Pisces
Height:	5' 8"-5' 10" (172-178cm)
Body Type:	Average
Looks:	Above average
Hair Colour:	Dark brown
Eye Colour:	Green
Ethnicity:	White/Caucasian
Home Language:	English
Other Languages:	French
Religion:	Christian/Catholic
Education:	Bachelor's degree
Occupation:	Self-employed
Income:	Enough
Drinking Habits:	Regular drinker
Smoking Habits:	Regular smoker
Relationship Status:	Single
Relationship Types:	Friends; Open to possibilities; Short-term; Long-term
Have Children:	No
Want Children:	No

His Narratives

Why should you get to know Narky?

You should get to know me because I am intelligent, funny, sincere, outgoing, unconventional and loads of other good things, but mostly because I am like nobody else you will ever meet. And mostly in a good way. *He describes his ideal match thus:*

You are confident, warm, attractive, witty, smart and fun to be with. You read. Books with words, that is, and not just *heat* magazine. You love movies. Real ones—ones with, wait for it, subtitles! Yes, foreign movies, like the ones they show in weird places like the IFI. You like a drink and a smoke, and are not freaked about the thoughts of going out on a school night. You are a current passport holder, and you use it regularly. You acknowledge all the crap stuff about Ireland as well as the good stuff. Owning a semi-d in Lucan and a new Micra equipped with two baby seats are not your ultimate life goals.

About His Ideal Match	
Country of Origin:	(Moderately important) Anywhere in Europe
Current Location:	(Moderately important) Dublin County (Dublin, Ireland)
Gender:	Female
Age Range:	(Decidedly important) 29—36
Has Photo:	Decidedly important
Recent Activity:	3 months
Star Sign:	Any
Height:	Any
Body Type:	(Decidedly important) Average
Looks:	(Decidedly important) Attractive
Hair Colour:	Any
Eye Colour:	Any
Ethnicity:	Any
Home Language:	(Moderately important) English
Other Languages:	Any
Religion:	Any
Education:	(Decidedly important) Bachelor's degree
Occupation:	Any
Income:	(Moderately important) Enough
Drinking Habits:	(Moderately important) Social drinker
Smoking Habits:	(Decidedly important) Regular smoker
Relationship Status:	(Non-negotiable) Single
Have Children:	(Decidedly important) No
Want Children:	(Moderately important) No

More About Him

More Physical Characteristics	
Hair Style:	Medium
Facial Hair:	I'm clean-shaven
Eyesight:	I've got 20/20 vision
Disabilities:	I have none
HIV Status:	Negative
Body Art:	I don't have any
Fashion Sense:	Casual (I'm usually in my favourite jeans)
Favourite Clothing:	My trusty pair of jeans

100

Personality Traits	
Personality Traits:	Easygoing; Funny; Intelligent; Outgoing; Outspoken; Sarcastic
Sense of Humour:	Sarcastic
Valued Qualities:	Contentment; Friendliness; Humility
Intelligence:	Intelligent
Ruled by:	The heart
Party Behaviour:	An impartial observer

Leisure & Entertainment	
Pastimes of choice:	Reading a book
Music Preferences:	Alternative; Blues; Classical; Dance/Disco; Rock
Reading:	I love it
Books:	Fiction; Non-fiction
TV Habits:	I don't have a TV
TV Shows:	Documentaries; Dramas
Movie Frequency:	It's a weekly ritual
Movie Preferences:	Art Films; Comedy; Cult Classics; Documentary; Independent
Take Drugs:	Socially

Dating & Relationships	
Current Relationship:	I'm single
Date Activities:	Walking on the beach

Sports, Hobbies & Interests	
Sport Involvement:	Watching from the sidelines
Sports:	Cycling; Tennis; Walking; Snooker
Interests:	Painting; Photography; Reading; Sculpting; Surfing the Internet; Woodworking; Writing books

Work & Lifestyle	
Pace of Life:	Hectic
Time at Work:	I work at home
Cooking:	I cook rather than starve
Dining Out:	I eat out a few times a week
Cuisine:	Doesn't matter
Family Size:	I've got brothers and sisters
Family Closeness:	We're dysfunctional
Time Online:	I'm on several hours a day

Likes & Dislikes	
Favourite Colour:	White
Animals:	I like animals
Pets (Like):	Dog(s); Horse(s)
Pets (Dislike):	Cat(s); Reptile(s); Rodent(s)
Turn-ons:	Assertiveness; Erotica; Flirting; Intelligence; Power; Sarcasm; Skinny-dipping; Thrill-seeking

Dreams, Aspirations & Goals	
Dream Home:	Beach house
Retirement Plans:	Sailing the seven seas

Philosophical Stuff	
Religious Attendance:	Rarely
Politics:	Liberal
Honesty:	Extremely

Mad, isn't it? I particularly liked the last question, which asked you to rate yourself on how honest you were when filling in the profile. Kinda takes you by surprise and may give those who were spoofing thus far pause for reflection. Profile done, photo uploaded, I did a quick search, requesting profiles of women aged between 29 and 36, resident anywhere in Europe. I got over 200 results and passed a pleasant hour or so sifting through them, checking out a few that looked interesting. As with DatingDirect, there were a good number of beautiful blondes from Russia and its neighbouring regions, so no doubt I'd be hearing from some of them, as was the case with the DatingDirect site in the UK. Refreshingly, most of the Irish girls on the site had a photo uploaded. Well, not most of them, but a good number anyway. Six of them were absolutely gorgeous, and even though I was happy enough with my progress to date, attacking on a number of fronts as I was, I couldn't resist sending a message to one delectable delight in the Midlands who caught my eye immediately. So hopefully, there'd be some news from her in the days to come.

I was just about to wrap things up when my e-mail notifier sounded its familiar alert and I saw a mail from my legal eagle,

Jane, in London. She was full of the joys of life, enjoying being caught up in some apparently complex, protracted, and no doubt highly profitable legal case, and making tentative enquiries as to when I might next be in London. (I had casually slipped in to one of my previous mails that I occasionally had 'business to attend to in the City', thereby legitimising my presence in the vicinity should I wish to take things further with herself or Rebecca. Which I didn't; at least not until I had played the Daisy Garnett hand to its fullest conclusion.) Anticipating that things with Daisy might move to the next level in the not too distant future, I bounced back a quick reply to Jane, telling her that she could indeed be lucky enough to meet me in a couple of weeks time. Positively exhausted from all my corresponding, I resolved to take a couple of days' leave from my online activities and chill out with a few movies and catch up on some reading[2] before heading off to Croatia.

---

2. Movie-wise I saw a couple of gems. *Comme Une Image,(Look at Me)*, directed by and starring Agnes Jaoui, is a terrific French film, featuring as it does the irrepressible Jean-Pierre Bacri. I was so impressed with the film that the following day I went straight down to Laser and rented Jaoui's previous film *Le Goût des Autres (It Takes All Sorts)*. Just as good. Terrible shame that at best .048% of you will probably ever see them—they knock spots off whatever opiate fodder is currently playing at your local multiplex.

Book-wise I flew through *'Treasures of the Deep: The Extraordinary Life & Times of Captain Mike Hatcher'* by Hugh Edwards, an amazing account of the life of renowned treasure hunter Mike Hatcher.

And I slept a lot. Very enjoyable few days. Sure, only a fool'd be working, as the man says.

11

The last week of July saw me returned from a glorious two weeks, which I had passed tucked away on a campsite on the Istrian peninsula in northern Croatia. Did quite a bit of driving around, but mostly I just slept and read loads of books on the beach. I did of course notify everyone concerned of my absence—didn't want them fretting over my lack of correspondence. When I arrived home in fine fettle (and quite tanned too I must add), I was ready to sally forth once again on the dating lark. A veritable bounty of e-mails had to be sifted through, though as it turned out, only a few were of genuine concern to me. Nothing from Daisy unfortunately, which was shame, but hopefully not the end of the matter by a long shot.

Talk about holding a candle though—Vera just wouldn't give up trying to win my heart. All very flattering and what have you, but my mind was made up—Daisy was the one for me. Until I changed my mind and developed a fixation on someone else at least. Vera's latest protestation of her undying love for me was, in fact, a little racy in places, so keen was she to get over here.[1] The

1. *Hello, my love, Donal.*

> *I love you and nothing make me forget you, my love, Donal. So be with me. My love, my tears in my eyes when I when I re-read*

1. *contd*

> *your message. I dream to be with you my love, I need you more than any time else. My love Donal, write to me. Do not forget me. Write that at you everything is all right. I very much worry.*
>
> *You, all my life will be for you. You want to take my soul to make you happy. I am ready to die for your happiness. I need you my dear. I will sacrifice all my life just to make you and me happy. Do not forget me, my love, Donal*
>
> *You forget all the hard conditions and sad things and begin a new life with happiness and love. I want to kiss you now but the kiss is not enough for me to express my love. I need me and you to be one. I want to give you a hug for many years to express my love. I need to hear your voice. I need to hear your voice, I need to see your face. I need you. I am afraid that one day you will forget our love and leave me. But I know that you will be with me forever. I need you to be with me in my life. Please, my love, Donal. Do not forget me, my love, Donal.*
>
> *I want you to take care of yourself. Please take care of yourself, my light. My dear Donal, this words is not just a speech but it is the deepest feelings I have ever felt towards any one. You are my prince, my life, my dear, my husband. Donal when I was in the darkness I saw in your eyes the light. When I was in sadness I found in your voice happiness, when I need someone beside me, I need you. When I wake up and found the sunrise late, I knew that the sunlight is asleep—you are the sunlight and you are the light of my life, my love, Donal.*
>
> *My dear Donal. All the words in the world mean nothing. I love you and all my life is nothing without you my love. My dear, my death is easier for me than if you leave me. Live for the hope of our meeting. Wait for me my dear and dream that our meeting will come soon. Do not forget me, my love, Donal*
>
> *All my hugs and my warm kisses for you my love. I kiss your lovely lips, I need to hold you in my arms and for me and you to be one person. I kiss you my prince Donal and am waiting for your messages.*
>
> *Your princess, Vera.*

In all fairness, you have to hand it to her—she did make a good case for shelling out a few hundred for a flight and a few start up incidentals. There's not too many attractive women out there these days who would declare—in writing, which I believe is quasi-contractual—that they're 'ready to die for your happiness' etc. I wondered what the Suffragettes would make of it all. And it was quite nice to be referred to as a 'prince' and 'the light' of someone's life, instead of a 'tit', or worse.

thing about it, though, was that it came nearly a full month after I decided not to respond to her previous message soliciting the transfer of funds to her account.[2] DatingDirect claimed to have literally thousands of registered members and to be largest internet dating provider in the UK, so the only logical conclusion is that I mustn't have been giving myself enough credit for how good a catch I really am.

Anyhoo, enough about Vera of Ryazan. One of the more promising e-mails awaiting my attention when I returned from Croatia was from Elaine. Elaine was one of the minxes on the Anotherfriend dating site that had been 'winking' at me flirtatiously, and to whom I responded with a few opening lines of interest. A flurry of short getting-to-know-you e-mails followed, along with an exchange of mobile telephone numbers—indicative of a degree of mutual interest in itself—and we spoke on the phone for the first time the day after I met Lisa, the IT girl. Elaine, 32, was a nurse, sorry, a matron, originally from Galway, but working in Dublin for the past few years, having previously done a stint in Dubai which had enabled her to buy an apartment in the city centre. She seemed to genuinely enjoy her job, something I found difficult to fathom, given the work involved and the chaotic state of the health service, but she seemed to be one of those people who was able to leave work at work and have a life outside of it.

She had a few days' leave to take and suggested we meet up one afternoon and just, 'Hang out, like, so there's no datey kind of

2. Much to Paul's dismay, I must add, when I rang him. He was all for getting her over on the plane.

'But Do, it's a readymade solution. It's worth thinking about.'

'No, it's a bit loopy in all fairness.'

'Not at all. Game, set and match is what is. Tell you what—I'll split the fare with you.'

'What? What are we gonna do? Share her?'

'No such luck—Rachel'd never go for that. Seriously, it'd be cool—just having a woman land on your doorstep, mad about you, ready to do whatever. If it doesn't work out, we can just send her back. No harm done.'

'Send her back? She's not a bloody toaster, you moron.'

The conversation ended shortly afterwards.

pressure, you know?' reasoning that if it was a complete disaster and we didn't hit it off we could each 'sod off home and get a DVD or something so the day wouldn't be a complete write-off'. I appreciated her candour and plans were made to meet outside the National Gallery. I'm not sure if people registered on Anotherfriend.com think that because Ireland is so small it would be all over the locality that so-and-so is a freak because they're using an internet dating service, but the vast majority of members have no photo accompanying their profile, so I had to settle for a few vague details from Elaine as to what she looked like.

Two-fifteen found me sitting on one of the benches outside the gallery on a mercifully pleasant day. I was just regretting not bringing a book with me to while away the hour or so late it looked like Elaine was going to be when a petite woman walked across the manicured square lawn, in flagrant breach of posted regulations and stood in front of me, hand across her forehead shielding her eyes from the intermittent sunshine.

'Are you Donal?' she asked directly.

'No, I'm not. Sorry,' I replied seriously.

'Oh shit, sorry. I was supposed to . . .' she said, turning to walk away.

'Only messing. I am. Elaine, hi,' I said smiling and standing to shake her hand.

'You gobshite! You had me mortified!' she shrieked, slapping my hand away.

'Sorry, I don't know why I did that. You looked like you could take a joke,' I offered by way of apology.

She shook her head and sat down on the bench I had just vacated, taking her denim day bag from over her shoulder and proceeded to rummage around inside.

'I need a cigarette now after that. And I'm supposed to be quitting,' she said without looking up at me, which gave me a chance to check her out properly. Cute, definitely cute, in that wholesome country way. Not necessarily the first one you'd pick out from a line-up maybe, but with one of those appearances that kind of grows on you. Slightly pale complexion, which was offset well by smooth longish black hair. Good skin, which is a must. Not too much make-up. Lovely eyes. Funky chick she was, too.[3]

'Aren't we all,' I replied, taking a seat beside her. 'Probably not such good idea to have a packet and a lighter on you then.' I suggested as she located her Marlboros (red too, if you don't mind—hardcore), and lit one up quickly, drawing satisfyingly on the long cancerous stem.

'Piss off,' she said nonchalantly. 'Today's an exceptional day.'

'I'm flattered,' I threw in.

'Get a grip,' she said smiling, 'not because of you—I wasn't that pushed about this to be honest—and you needn't think you're getting a ride later on either, so you can put any thoughts of that out of your filthy mind now, do you hear me?' she continued seriously.

We've got a live one here and no doubt about it, I was thinking. Not five minutes into it and she's shooting from the hip. Telepathic too. I said nothing and just started laughing, taking the opportunity to light a cigarette of my own.

'Don't flatter yourself. Who says I'd want to shag you?' I said a minute later, upping my game to match her feisty opening salvo.

'You're a man, aren't you?' Elaine half sneered.

'Jesus, are you always this much fun?' I joked. 'People say I'm a cynic, but you're on a whole other level altogether. So why is today an exceptional day then?'

'I'm not cynical at all, just letting you know the way it's going to be,' she said matter-of-factly. 'And it just is. I might tell you later on if you're good.'

'Fair enough,' I said casually, not wanting to let on that I was interested, when in fact I was.

We went into the gallery and wandered around. We were chatting away no problem, but it was as if we were two people who had just met by chance, and each of us was at something of a loose end for a couple of hours and had decided to hang out with the other as an alternative to killing time on our own. I got the feeling Elaine felt the same way. In other words, neither of us was what the other was looking for.

3. Original Converse boots, faded jeans, plain white T-shirt (quite tight too, revealing a pleasing array of curves in all the right places), and combat jacket. Pretty cool for a 32-year-old, I thought.

And so we strolled on through a few of the galleries, stopping to look at whatever interested us. Went in to the new wing then, which was much busier with lots of tourists and pensioners milling around. I've no idea what the fuss about that place is: you'd swear people had never seen an atrium before. We had a look in a few of the rooms but we'd both seen most of it before and decided to go to the café and be robbed blind for dry pastries and inferior coffee.

'Pathetic the way people give a few quid to towards the construction of these places on condition that their name's plastered all over the place, isn't it?' I said as we finally found a table in the noisy café.

'Better than them not giving it though, isn't it?' Elaine countered.

'Not really. It's not the like the place wouldn't have been built. It's just vanity. People are much more generous once they're assured that the nation will be aware of their generosity. They probably get a tax credit for it too.'

'I couldn't care less anyway,' she said breezily. 'It's their money and they can do what they like with it. And who knows, if they didn't give it, maybe there'd be a shortfall and you'd end up paying an admission fee to drink shite coffee in here.'

'Yeah, that wouldn't be cool at all. Listen, I was wondering if you could clear something up for me. When we were in college we were always wondering what the deal was with nurses, you know? The way everyone says they're easy and what not? And our theory was that . . .'

'What are you like? Are you a complete moron?' Elaine interrupted.

'Wait a second, hear me out. We spent a lot of time on this,' I continued. 'We reckoned that because they worked in such close proximity to death all the time, coupled with the fact they've such a handy job, you know, a week on and a week off kind of thing, that when they went out on the town, they were game for a laugh because they were all too aware of the fragility of human life and what have you, and that they'd be of the we're-here-for-a-good-time-not-a-long-time frame of mind. What do you think? As someone on the inside, like? Does it hold water?'

Elaine shook her head sadly and took a moment to reflect. 'My God, you actually *are* a complete moron. It's amazing. You don't look it, but you are.'

'What? We were in first year in college. It was a dump—no facilities, shit lecturers, no pool table, zero talent. What else were we supposed to do?'

'Study, maybe?'

'In first year? No need. Cram for a few days and you're sorted. So? What do you make of our theory?'

'I think it's fundamentally flawed, disrespectful to women in general, nurses in particular and indicative of how pathetic men are at their core. It's also of some concern to me specifically in that I currently find myself sitting beside an idiot who is apparently quite happy to acknowledge his part in its formulation,' Elaine replied eloquently, barely suppressing a smile.

'Great the way we clicked isn't it?' I said smiling. 'I thought it might be a bit awkward meeting you, that we wouldn't have a whole lot to say, but this is going grand, isn't it?'

'It's not the worst,' Elaine conceded magnanimously. 'How long are you on the website?'

'Only a couple of months. I was away for a while though, so I'm only really getting stuck into it now. How about you?'

'Six months now.'

'Really? And how many dates have you been on?'

'Loads. Well, about nine or ten.'

'Shit, nine or ten dates in six months. That's a lot really when you think about it. Starting from scratch every time. And did you always take the initiative? You know, like you did with me, sending out an old wink and what have you?'

'I'm starting to regret that now. And no, I didn't. You're actually the first person I did that to. All the others got in touch with me or sent me a wink.'

'Oh yeah? And how did the dates go? Not great obviously if you're still at it, I suppose?'

'Smartarse. Some of them were actually very enjoyable. All nice enough lads, went out with one or two them a couple of times.

Just didn't connect enough with any of them to make me want to make the effort, you know?'

'Did you shag any of them?' I asked casually.

Elaine met me with a blank stare.

'What? I'm only asking. You don't have to answer if you don't want to.'

'No I didn't. Not that it's any of your business,' she answered curtly.

'There goes our theory so,' I laughed. 'I know what you mean though. If there's one thing I can't stand doing, it's making an effort. The effort of it all is just too much. Because for me, there should be no effort required. If you meet someone and they're totally cool, and you're mad about them, then that situation requires no effort because you *want* to be with them and you *want* to include them in your life and all that, so it doesn't feel like you're making special accommodation for them. But if you actually *feel* that you're making an effort to be with them, then you know it's all wrong and it's never going to work out.'

'Words of wisdom, huh?' Elaine asked sarcastically.

'I'm telling you, that's the way it is. For me anyway.

'And how long have you been single, pray tell?'

'Fair enough, I've been single more than not. But really, up until now I just couldn't be arsed, to be honest with you. If I met someone and something happened, cool. If I didn't, then that was cool too. I've always had plenty to keep me occupied. But now all my friends are married so they're not allowed out a whole lot, and when they are the conversation inevitably turns to the prohibitive cost of childcare or how to maximise the tax relief on a company car, both subjects not relevant to my situation. So I thought it'd be handy to have a girlfriend for a while and see how it goes, you know?'

'*Handy?* It'd be *handy* to have a girlfriend? How romantic.'

'Well, you know. For going out during the week, seeing a movie or a grabbing a bit of dinner. Or slipping off to Copenhagen for a weekend and what have you: I hate getting fleeced for single supplements. It's so discriminatory. Like you've no entitlement to go away if you're single.'

'With that reasoning it's truly amazing you haven't been snapped up,' Elaine said acerbically. 'How about falling in love and wanting to share your life with someone?'

'Oh yeah, that's cool and the gang. But that'll happen if it's supposed to happen. You can't make yourself fall in love with someone just because you're getting older. It's different for women though, with the kids thing and all that. What age are you again? Thirty-two? Yeah, you'd want to be getting a move on I suppose, wouldn't you?'

'God Almighty, you're unreal,' she sighed, reaching across the table to give me a slap. 'Come on, let's go, the excitement here is killing me.'

Back out in the late-afternoon sunshine, we wandered aimlessly up towards Grafton Street, arguing about what to do next. Elaine suggested going to a movie but I had to veto it on what she thought were pathetically nebulous grounds.[4] She then suggested a drink and maybe a bite to eat later on if I hadn't annoyed her too much by then. (She was only joking though, I was sure of it. I thought we were getting on great.) So we argued for another little bit about which pub to go to, each of us stridently making the case for our preferred watering hole. She was a Keogh's fan, which was fair enough, it's a cool pub. But there's nowhere to sit outside if you want to have a smoke, whereas Bruxelles, just around the corner, has ample outside seating, under a canopy in case it starts to rain, gas heaters in case it gets cold, *and* the jukebox has great tunes on it. Technically, the last one doesn't qualify if you're outside smoking because the jukebox is downstairs and you wouldn't be able to hear said tunes, but still, I thought it was a point in its favour. She eventually capitulated and ten minutes later we were ensconced at a table outside one of the last few genuinely cool pubs in Dublin, watching the world go by and taking turns to make completely unfounded and unreasonable comments on all who passed before us.

4. The film Elaine wanted to see was on in the UGC multiplex, and I only give my celluloid custom to the Screen cinema—my favourite place in Dublin city—and, on occasion, the Irish Film Institute. Nebulous? I think not.

'So where are you taking me for dinner?' she said after we debated the sexual orientation of a courier proudly adjusting the package bulging out of his Lycra shorts before mounting his chariot outside the offices in front of us.

'The Market Bar,' I replied straight away. 'It's great.'

'I bet you say that to all the girls,' she said, draining her pint of Guinness.

'I do actually. I couldn't be arsed trying to think of anywhere else to go. Unless someone else is paying for it, I don't really go in for the whole dining out thing, it's normally such a let-down. I was in there a while ago actually—on another date with this girl Lisa—and guess what she tells me?'

'That you're a complete tit and she never wanted to see you again?' Elaine ventured.

'Not exactly, no. That she was pregnant! Can you believe that?' I said, getting up from the table.

'What's wrong with that?'

'Duh! Pregnant. With child. And there she was on a date with me, eight weeks gone, like. I couldn't believe it. I was a bit narked she hadn't told me before we'd arranged to meet up to be honest, but . . .'

'Why? Would you not have gone?' Elaine asked as we set off on the short walk to the bar.

'Maybe not. It's a bit odd, in all fairness. Although I would have been intrigued to know the story behind it, all right. She wasn't a scrubber or anything, quite the opposite in fact. Little IT dynamo. Sells servers. Lots of them apparently. Turned out to be a good old night at the end of it.'

'Are you going to see her again?'

'No. Not on a date anyway. She was cool enough now, I have to say. Quite cute too, but I think she's looking for a nice guy to settle down with and . . .'

'And you don't fit the bill.'

'No, I don't. But we got on grand. We'll keep in touch, I think. Might meet for a coffee sometime or something.'

The Market Bar was pretty busy but we got a table and ordered quickly. Elaine had said she was starving and was going for the chicken brochettes so I suggested she order a large portion. Our food arrived shortly after and we tucked in greedily. Elaine was a good eater, something I like to see in a woman. I hate these ones who are so insecure they just order a salad so their date doesn't think they eat like a horse and will end up really fat. We chatted away happily throughout the meal and then repaired to the archway for a cigarette and another drink.

As it neared seven o'clock I was kind of wishing we had met a little later in the day instead of just after lunch, because things between us were warming up nicely I thought. If we had met at say, five or six and had the crack we'd had thus far, I think it's fair to say that a taxi might have been called and who knows what would have happened then. As it stood, I felt that we were getting close to the point where we might be running out of steam for our first meeting and it was way too early to be making any soundings about whose place we should head to for a nightcap and what have you. I decided to play it cool and see if Elaine took the initiative.

'What time is it?' she said after a minute or so of pleasant silence.

'It's, ah, nearly seven,' I said, pretending to check the clock on my phone. 'Why?'

'I'd better be heading off soon. I said I'd meet a friend for a drink. She's off on holidays tomorrow so I won't see her for a while.'

'Oh, right. And what about this?' I asked, gesturing with my hand at the space between us.

'What's *this*, exactly?' said Elaine, smiling, repeating my gesture mockingly.

'*This*, you know. Do you want to hook up again or do you want to move on to date number seventeen?'

'Eleven, actually. And I'll let you know,' she said, all cocky, as she stubbed out her cigarette and got her bag.

'Fair enough. I won't hold my breath,' I replied lightheartedly, moving a stool out of her way.

'You're an interesting guy, Donal. Hard work, no doubt, but you're interesting. I'm not sure that we're on the same page, though, in terms of what we're looking for, you know? You seem to be out there trying this whole relationship thing out to see what it's like, and that's fine. But I'm kinda ready for a bit more than that. No guarantee I'll find it, but there you go. Do you know what I mean?' she explained as we stood on the corner of George's Street before we went our separate ways, her north and me south.

'Yeah, sure, that's cool, I know where you're coming from. Listen Elaine, I had a great day anyway, I'm glad we did it. I don't really do the whole wooing thing unless I know it'll be reciprocated so I'll leave it to you to do a postmortem with your friends and if you decide you could stick it out again, maybe I'll hear from you, yeah? And if not, no problem. You wouldn't be the first to make the mistake of a lifetime,' I said smiling.

'Maybe I'll regret it for the rest of my life,' Elaine said in a rueful tone, leaning in to give me a quick kiss on the cheek. 'I don't think so, but you never know. Bye.'

And she was gone. Never found out what was exceptional about her day either.

———

'You're kidding me?' Paul said incredulously when I rang him later. 'No back to hers, no?'

'No, she wasn't up for it. All on for meeting Mr Right.'

'What about our theory?'

'Yeah, I gave her that, but she wasn't having any of it. Said I was a moron. Can you believe that?'

'That's not cool, in all fairness. Gonna have to work on our finishing, though. We need points on the board soon, Do. What's the story with the away fixture? Any word from London town?'

'No, not yet. Don't know what the deal is with Daisy. You'd think she'd have been on the phone by now.'

'Yeah. We'll see. How are you fixed for the qualifiers?'

'The what?'

'The speed dating thing.'

'Oh, right. Ah, yeah, grand. You never know with these things—all depends on who's there on the night.'

'Totally. Listen, better go. It's kicking off here—I'm late with the bottle.'

'Right so. Good luck.'

12

Speed dating—two hundred single women in a room; a few drinks in them; and they *have* to talk to you. Had to be worth a shot, I'd thought when I'd rather rashly registered for it. Three hours after the event, I realised that I would have sooner shot myself in the head. Complete. And utter. Trag. Edy.

It was a warm balmy Saturday evening and the venue was the Alexander Hotel. 'Chatfest' was the name given to the event by the organisers, in an effort to distinguish it from the myriad number of speed-dating-type events taking place all over the city on what seemed like an hourly basis. To avoid looking like a complete reject going into the place on my own I decided that I needed a wingman. I lucked out, though, and got a wingwoman. Not just any old wingwoman either, but Sue, a good friend of mine who was home from Australia for a couple of weeks.

In terms of an overall package, Sue is categorically the coolest chick I have ever met. Apart from being gorgeous, she has a dyna-mite personality, is outrageously intelligent, emotionally mature, smiles with her heart, doesn't take any crap from anyone, and most of the time seems to have genuinely no idea how devastatingly attractive she is. In short, she is, quite literally, an extraordinary woman. Her only failing, and it is quite a significant one, is thus far not realising that I'm her perfect match. Not because I mirror her in possession of the above attributes—I don't—but because I recognise them to a greater degree than anyone else does. That's not to say that she doesn't have her suitors, she does, legions of them, but they're just not right for her. Not the way I am. Still, only six more years to go and then she's mine.[1]

I met Sue outside the train station around the corner from the hotel and we decided to get a drink before going in. I hadn't seen her in ages—I had actually seen her two days previously but before that it had been nearly a year since we'd met—and we were yapping away about this and that, catching up on gossip and regaling each other with dramatic episodes from our recent pasts, when it struck me that without even seeing the two hundred women in the hotel around the corner, the best date I could hope to have that night was Sue. As could only be the way with her, we were no sooner in the bar than she met someone she knew from bloody Sydney—I could walk around town butt naked for an afternoon and not meet anybody I know. We had a drink with them and then headed across the road into the unknown.

There were quite a few people milling around the lobby of the hotel, and it has to be said, a lot of the women were very attractive. Given that Sue was out of bounds for another four years, 186 days and four hours, give or take, I decided to make an effort and be at my most charming for the evening. We went downstairs to register and were presented with name tags, pens and a piece of paper by the scarily enthusiastic coordinators. I'm sure you know the drill: people put the name tag on their shirts so they don't waste valuable seconds from their four-minute allocation asking someone what their name is, and the pen and paper is for ticking off the names of those people you liked and who you wouldn't mind seeing again on a proper date.

By this stage there was a large crowd around us waiting to sign in so Sue and I decided to adjourn to the bar upstairs for a drink before the proceedings got under way. As we made our way up the

1. Sue and I made an agreement a while back that if we're both still single by the time we're 40, we'll just call it a day and hook up. As an aside, I've been reading a lot about developments in the field of time travel recently.

stairs a group of lads were coming down to register and as we passed, one of them quipped, 'This'll be deadly, he's scored already'. I wish. As the kick-off neared, Sue started to get a little giddy and I was hoping she'd back out and that we could sod off and spend the night together, but she settled herself with the aid of a swift cocktail of Australian origin, the name of which I won't repeat in case her mother reads this.

Eight o'clock came and everyone descended to the conference room downstairs. There were four long tables laid out side by side, each accommodating 50 people, 25 guys and 25 girls. The delirious coordinators led everyone to their places at the different tables, smiling demonically as they did so, like we were all part of some big joke and only they knew the punchline. I was escorted to a table at the far end of the room and was somewhat disappointed to see Sue at the next table to me.

I took one look down the opposite side of my table at the women awaiting my chat and every fibre of my being told me to run for my life. Where were all the honeys from the bar upstairs? And through what basement entrance had these trolls slipped in? What the hell was going on? Someone call security! I took a look around the room and sure enough, the honeys were all at the other tables. I had another look at the yokes at my table and realised that they were the oldest women in the room. The logistics of trying to ensure that every man spoke to every one of the two hundred women there were too much to contemplate, so the organisers had divided us up on the basis of age, ensuring that every man and every woman would spend four or five minutes chatting to 25 people in the same age bracket as themselves. But if that was the case, why wasn't Sue at my table? She won't thank me for saying this, but she's the same age as me. I looked around and tried to catch her attention, but some sleazy Lothario was already trying his luck with her. I got up and went over to her chair. When she saw my ashen face she covered her mouth and tried not to laugh. 'What's the matter, darling?' she asked tenderly, like she didn't know.

'What's the matter? I'll tell you what the matter is. Look at my table. Look at the yokes I'm landed with. Why aren't you over there? Did you lie about your age?'

'Of course I lied about my age. Look at the muppets at your table. What makes you think I'd want to talk to them?' she said, amazed I hadn't thought this through more carefully myself.

'But I want to be at your table, look at all the cute chicks you've got. Mine looks like some single parents' support group,' I moaned.

'Okaaaaay! Are we ready?' the ringmaster shouted, seemingly forgetting he had a megaphone at the end of his gob which obviated the need for doing just that. 'Everybody take your seat. Your allocated seat, I might add, no last-minute changing around,' he continued, reading my mind.

'Shit.'

'Best of luck, darling,' Sue said sweetly, turning to face her suitors, apparently keen to get going. 'See you at the interval.'

'If I last that long,' I said dejectedly, sloping off towards my seat.

Our MC ran through the procedure: four minutes' chat with your opposite number, and when the horn sounded, all the men would stand up and move down one seat to their right. There'd be a break after we had each spoken to twelve people and then we'd resume for the second leg. After that, everybody was to hand back his/her sheets of paper (we could keep the pens), so that the 'matches' could be tallied. Everybody would receive an e-mail in a few days' time letting them know how many, if any, of the people they had ticked as having taken their fancy had also ticked them. Mobile numbers and e-mail addresses would then be exchanged and everyone could go off and break each other's heart. Simple.

Date 1.
Short, blonde highlighted hair. Rosy-red cheeks. (From alcohol, not going OTT with the rouge.) Wearing, I kid you not, her best and shiniest track suit bottoms and a white sports T-shirt. Forty if she was a day. I'm not saying she was big, but . . .[2] Pleasant enough woman, salt of the earth and all that, but separated with an eleven-year-old son? No tick.

2. I could have sworn she was sitting on two chairs, one for each of the twins, if you know what I mean.

Date 2.

Long brown hair. Dark eyes. Mortgage lending officer. Looked aghast when I told her I didn't own my own home. Nearly fell over when I said I'd had three but sold them to make a crap movie a few years back. No tick.

Date 3.

Thirty-six—told me straight out, like it was something she just had come to terms with. Pleasant enough to look at in a wallflower-type of way. Long dark hair, green eyes, good skin. Reckoned she had the potential to be wild in bed. Certified cost accountant.[3] Started to twitch nervously when I told her I was a writer. No tick.

Date 4.

Short black hair, worn like there was no mirror in her house. Teacher. Scribbled notes constantly like she was grading book reports. Engaged twice. Looking to 'settle down'. Maybe if she looked at someone when they were talking to her she'd have more luck. No tick.

Date 5.

Blonde. Blue eyes. Nice smile. Well dressed. Doctor. Asked me if I smoked. I said yes. Told me about the risk of contracting cancer at my age. No tick.

Date 6.

Mid-thirties. Small with pale complexion. Short black wiry hair. Glasses stolen from Deirdre Barlow. Looked more excited at the prospect of having twenty-five *people*, never mind men, talk to her than could possibly be justified. I'm not saying she was boring but I fell asleep twice in the four minutes. No tick.

Date 7.

Brown hair, green eyes. Great body. Very revealing top. Deep tan, albeit from a bottle/bed. Self-absorbed, vain cow. Kept toying with her necklace, hoping I'd ask her where she got it.[4] Worked in her father's travel agency; i.e. she didn't work at all. Just broke up

---

3. Changed my mind about the wild-in-bed thing when I heard that.

4. 'Oh this thing? The Maldives, I think it was.'

with long-term boyfriend and wanted to 'have some fun'. I said something mildly amusing. She laughed disproportionately. Knew I could do better. Strong possibility of a rebound shag, I thought. Tick.

Date 8.

Thirty-two. (Skewed the mean age at our table by 14.6 %.) From Galway originally. Moving back to Galway imminently once she got planning permission for a site her father had given her. Teacher. Said she loved 'good movies, you know? Really good ones.' I listed five great movies.[5] She'd only seen one of them. No tick.

Date 9.

Only had a minute with her as the chap next to me couldn't bring himself to leave her and move on. I coughed politely a few times and he eventually moved down, only to continue wooing her from the next seat, leaving me and his intended date to look bemusedly at each other as the star-crossed lovers finished talking. Finally got her alone and asked her what they were talking about. Golf. No tick.

Date 10.

Knew I didn't like her straight away. Narky looking cow, like she resented having to be there, amazed she hadn't been snapped up by some blind, deaf mute. Passed a disinterested minute or so talking about the antics of the other pair and then just looked at each other until the horn sounded. What do you think?

Date 11.

Married. Separated for two years. 'What happened?' 'None of your business.' Major issues. No tick.

Date 12.

Attractive looking woman, holding up well for her late thirties. Lovely eyes and a great smile. Warm personality. Shook my hand when she introduced herself. Didn't seem put out by my not

---

5. *Magnolia, The Straight Story, Three Colours Trilogy, Requiem for a Dream,* and *Adaptation* were the movies I mentioned. The only one she'd seen was *Adaptation*—'I looove Nicolas Cage.' I generally can't stand him, but he is great in it.

having a 'proper' job. Last book read was Jeffrey Eugenides' *Middlesex*, on holidays in France. Interesting, if only by virtue of her rarity value amongst the other lot. Tick.

Interval. Thank God.

'This is great, isn't it?' shrieked Sue, as we rejoined in the hallway outside.

'We're leaving,' I said solemnly, taking her upstairs and outside for some fresh air and a smoke.

'Why? Are you not having a good time at your table?' she asked innocently, smiling flirtatiously to one of her suitors as we passed him in the lobby.

'No, I'm not. It's incredibly depressing,' I replied, giving her a rundown of what I'd just been through.

She, on the other hand, had sat at her table, a queen without a crown, and had guy after guy tell her all manner of complimentary things about her—all of which were true no doubt—and was particularly taken with some French dude who had kissed her hand as he was leaving her. We went back in to the bar for a drink and she agreed to leave if I really wanted to, but said I had to make up my mind quickly because if we were going, she wanted to 'say goodbye to a few people' first and give them her number. I reminded her of the futility of such an exercise in light of the fact that she was returning to Australia in two weeks' time, and also of the fact that she was present at the event primarily as a peripheral figure, as my wingwoman, and was not necessarily supposed to be having a good time. She laughed haughtily and said she'd get another drink in before we went back down, timing her confident stride to the bar in line with Henri's approach towards us. She pretended to be talking to me over her shoulder as she sashayed across the floor, deliberately bumping into the Frenchman, and then paused to excuse herself coquettishly, allowing him the opportunity to chat her up again, which he seized immediately and which she relished. God, she was good.

I decided to go back downstairs and see just how bad things would get in the second leg. Our MC kicked things off again, telling us that after the event was finished we were all to go onto a club in the city centre and dance the night away with our new friends. I looked dubiously across at Sue and she gave me a deadly serious thumbs-up. No more cocktails for her. The horn sounded and the deafening clamour of four hundred semi-inebriated singletons resumed.

Date 13.

I didn't say a whole lot to my thirteenth date, principally because she wasn't there. I spent three minutes and forty-two seconds staring at an empty chair, breathing deeply and consciously asserting my will to live. She scuttled in eventually, apologising breathlessly for being late. We said hello and the horn sounded. Great body. What the hell. Tick.

Date 14.

Married. Happily. And a ring on her finger to prove it. Said she just came in 'for the laugh' with a friend of hers who was desperate to meet someone. Unbelievable. No tick, obviously.

Date 15.

The desperate friend of Date 14. I could see why. No tick.

Date 16.

A really lovely woman. Not my bag in terms of looks at all, but a really sound, genuine woman who was just looking to meet a regular guy. I'm sure I did no more for her than she did for me, but I gave her a confidence-boosting tick anyway. It's the kind of guy I am.

Date 17.

Touch of ocp[6] about this one. Kept adjusting the position of her pen to make sure it was exactly parallel to the top of her piece of paper and that the paper was in turn parallel to the edge of the table. Also

6. ocp: Obsessive Compulsive Disorder. Defined by the us National Library of Medicine as 'an anxiety disorder characterized by obsessions or compulsions. Having one or both is sufficient for the diagnosis. An obsession is a recurrent and intrusive thought, feeling, idea, or sensation. A compulsion is a conscious, recurrent pattern of behavior a person feels driven to perform. This behavior can be a physical action (such as recurrent handwashing), or a mental act (such as praying, repeating words silently, counting). The behavior is aimed at neutralising anxiety or distress.'

seemed concerned about the hygiene standards of the four-star hotel we were in and wiped the glass the waiter brought her vigorously before filling it with her wine. Amusing to watch certainly, but you couldn't be dealing with that on a regular basis. No tick.

Date 18.

Hardly got a word in with this one. She was obviously very nervous and kept talking non-stop for about three minutes flat. About her job and her new house and her dog. Who was called Spot if you can believe it. Ironically so, apparently, 'because he doesn't have any!' She was a ticket and no mistake. Counted down the seconds until the horn sounded. No tick.

Date 19.

Was feeling weary now, and only the sight of the end of the table nearing kept me there. This one was sending a text message as I sat down, so I made a quip about how difficult it must be juggling all the men in her life. Response: 'I was actually just texting my babysitter, if you must know'. Well able to take a joke. No tick.

Date 20.

Felt a hand on my shoulder as I sat down. It was Sue, who whispered to me that she'd she meet me outside in two minutes. There was a God! I nonchalantly told my date I had to go to the bathroom and got up from my chair. She didn't seem impressed at all, but I just grabbed my jacket and split, handing my piece of paper to one of the by-now-fatigued coordinators as I left.

I met Sue upstairs in the lobby and was delighted to see that the sparkle was gone out of her eyes and that she looked seriously pissed off.

'What's up, babe?' I asked as she raised her eyes heavenward and made for the door.

'Nothing but rejects for the last twenty minutes. I couldn't take any more,' she moaned.

'Now you know how I felt at my table,' I said. 'It was a complete disaster. I'm never doing anything like this again. Going out on the pull in a bar is better than this shit.'

'Oh, God, Do, are we really bad for just leaving like that?' wondered Sue.

'Load of shite that was, I've a good mind to go down and look for a refund,' some lad wailed behind us, pulling his jacket on disgustedly as his two friends nodded in sombre agreement.

'No we're not,' I assured her. 'There were far too many people there for it to have any chance of working out. Whoever was running that thing tonight must have cleared about €7,000. And that division-by-age thing was a load of rubbish. Everyone knows that men are such saps it takes them a few years longer than women to cop on and sort themselves out. Look at the vast majority of couples and you'll see the guy is a couple of years older than the girl. It was a shambles,' I ranted. 'Come on, let's get a drink.'

'I need a cocktail,' Sue said dramatically.

'Me too.'

At least one of my dates turned out well.

———

Paul wasn't impressed.

'You're kidding me. You left early? That's not the way, Do. We could have got a late goal, you never know,' he said testily.

'No chance, sure I could see what was ahead of me. Just couldn't take it any more,' I replied wearily.

'This is a disaster. We're heading for relegation at this rate.'

'Thanks for the vote of confidence.'

'Ah, no, I'm with you all the way. We just need a result though, you know? Be good for morale.'

'Tell me about it.'

'I'm under serious pressure here, Do. Rachel said I should get rid of you on a free transfer,' he said gravely.

'She said that?'

'Well, not in those words exactly. She said you're a tit and that any woman in their right mind would run a mile from you.'

'Lovely. Tell her I said hi. How's the baby?'

'Great. He'll be on solids soon enough, the way he's going. He's massive.'

13

I had still not heard from Daisy again before I went on the speed dating travesty, so I sent her another e-mail, promising myself that this would be the last. However attractive she may have been, if she was too ignorant to reply politely to a response I had sent to *her* e-mail, then good luck to her. In the message I let it be known that I had business to attend to in London in a couple of weeks and that it would be great if we could meet for a drink or a bite to eat. Obviously, I had no business to attend to in London, or anywhere else for that matter, but I didn't want her to think that I had no business to attend to in London, or anywhere else for that matter, in case she thought that I was travelling to London solely to see her. Which I was.

If there was no response from her this time, I'd leave well enough alone. I had wooed her from afar and sent her a beautiful and thoughtful gift. The least I expected was an affectionate and grateful response, and I got that. Admittedly, I felt there was an undertone of reciprocation implicit in her thank-you note, and in hindsight—which isn't worth a damn really because it's wisdom is received after that point in time when you could benefit from it— maybe I got a little carried away with myself. Still, no harm done. Not yet, anyway. Didn't want her suggesting I was harassing her—

the last thing I needed was a repeat of the whole Tania Bryer affair.[1]

1. You might remember the delightful Tania Bryer from your television screens some years ago. In 1988, as preparations were being finalised for our debutante ball at school, the thorny issue of who should escort me to the function arose. Needless to say, I was single at the time, and had been flitting between not going at all one week and then going the next. I decided to go, once-in-a-lifetime event and all that, and then decided that the Number One candidate on my shortlist of prospective partners for the evening could only be Ms Tania Bryer, a very attractive weather presenter I had become somewhat infatuated with. Though I knew her only from her appearances on the television, I felt confident enough about her accepting the invitation with the good grace she seemed to convey when presenting the following day's meteorological report to me every evening: genuinely saddened at having to announce the likelihood of rain with a possibility of localised flooding and positively euphoric at being able to confirm long periods of hazy sunshine.

   And so, after some investigation to ascertain her contact details within the organisation where she worked, a comprehensive letter and invitation were dispatched. A period of two weeks elapsed—ample time I thought to allow for the delivery of the letter, due consideration of its contents and subsequent dispatch of her delighted acquiescence to the invitation. However, with no reply, affirmative or otherwise, forthcoming, I decided to call her directly at her place of work. International directory enquiries were consulted and the relevant number obtained. After much to-ing and fro-ing between different extensions and departments, I was finally put through to an associate of Ms Bryer. Loath as I was to divulge the somewhat intimate nature of my reasons for wishing to speak with her, this associate made it pointedly clear that Ms Bryer was a very busy woman and that all external communications for her attention must pass through her. I vaguely outlined the nature of my invitation, left a contact telephone number and politely requested Ms Bryer call me as soon as she could. I thought I heard what sounded like a barely stifled chortle on the other end, but put it down to interference on the line.

   A few days passed, and still no reply. Berating the associate's incompetence, I called again, fully intent on speaking to a superior to voice a sternly worded complaint about the associate's complete failure to carry out her duties—why else could there have been no reply from Ms Bryer?—and to suggest that disciplinary measures be taken in the light of such wanton insubordination. My recriminations

A few days passed and still no word from Ms Garnett. I got to thinking that perhaps she was something of a fake. Whilst on the one hand she seemed to profess a taste for the adventurous, the unexpected and seemed open to new encounters, I suspected that what she was really looking for was a malleable man. A wealthy, malleable man, who could keep her in the style she aspired to, so that when she next set off across a desert or an ocean, it would be in the lap of luxury, with no worries about budgetary constraints.

I had, somewhat presumptuously it now appeared, already booked a flight and accommodation for the night, and obviously didn't want them to go to waste so I decided to give Jane a ring and see if she was up to meeting for a coffee or dinner. I got through to her messaging system and let her know my plans, expecting, and hoping for, a swift reply. With none forthcoming within the hour I decided to go out on a limb and give my Rebecca a shout as well. I knew the likelihood of anything happening between us was remote to say the least, but we had been keeping in touch, bouncing friendly and innocuous e-mails across the water with some regularity.

She answered on the second ring with a bright but terribly Sloane Ranger accent. Thankfully, when I introduced myself, her finishing-school etiquette kicked in and she was very friendly. I told her about the pressing business I had to attend to in London, but said I would be free from about noon if she fancied meeting for lunch or a coffee. After only a slight pause and a playful little

1. *contd* would be followed by a request that, in view of the breakdown of communications within the organisation, I be put through to Ms Bryer directly. Amazingly, on all counts, my requests were tersely denied. As if that wasn't bad enough, a registered letter duly arrived some three days later, from the Human Resources Manager of the organisation no less, stating that if I did not immediately desist with my 'unsolicited and wholly unwelcome' attempts to communicate with Ms Bryer, to whom I had allegedly caused 'great distress and emotional upset', a file on the matter would be sent to Scotland Yard. Stupefied at the arrogance of the woman, I proceeded in a southerly direction to the second candidate on my shortlist.*

    * Incidentally, I ended up attending the function with the fourth candidate on the shortlist.**

    ** The shortlist contained four candidates.

giggle she said she'd 'love to'. She was 'terribly busy' at work, but said she could 'do' a quick lunch and suggested Isola, in Kinghtsbridge—of course. All business, she offered to book a table for two, for one. Then she asked what was bringing me to London, so I gave her a line about having to meet an agent about possible UK representation, which she declared 'terribly exciting'. (I would have agreed wholeheartedly if I had any such meeting to attend.) We chatted for a little while before Rebecca rung off, saying she was just back from the gym and starving.

She did sound 'terribly' pleasant, polite and what have you but I got the feeling that our assignation might be a little strained after twenty minutes or so, by which time I reckoned we would have exhausted all conversational options open to us. What the hell— I'd never see her again if I didn't want to, and I was glad I'd made the call anyway.

I had just settled down on the sofa to watch *Mulholland Drive*— again—when my mobile rang. It was Jane, returning my call excitedly, saying that dinner sounded like a great idea. Apparently, she was wrapping up some complex and protracted case and was dying for a break. I told her I had a meeting in the afternoon but that I'd be free from about four onwards (giving myself ample time to entertain Rebecca). Jane's office was near Covent Garden so she suggested meeting first in a nearby bar called Bacchanalia, and that we could go on from there for a bite to eat. Sounded good to me, so I said I'd see her there at six, and we rang off.

Never rains but it pours.[2] It's great when the woman chooses the venue, too—I can't then be held responsible for crap food or poor service or whatever else may put a damper on the proceedings. Looking forward to my day of power-dating in London town, I made a quick note of the details and pressed 'play' once again.

———

2. Paul's mood lifted considerably when I told him of my forthcoming trip:

'That's great news, Do. Just what we need mid-season—a double header. No messing around with this pair now, get stuck in.'

I strolled into Oliver Peyton's chic Isola restaurant at 12.55 the following Wednesday afternoon, Rebecca's photo from the website etched on the back of my retinas—didn't want to want to walk right past her like a fool, or have her scanning the place anxiously trying to spot me. It was fairly busy with a mostly young, conspicuously trendy crowd, most of them desperately keen to be seen and heard by everyone else on the premises. Delighted to find Rebecca already seated at a table—most unusual for a woman to be early, I thought—I strolled boldly over to her and extended a hand.

'Rebecca, hi. Donal. Lovely to meet you at last,' I said warmly.

'Donal. Hello,' she said politely, her brain synapses instructing a warmish smile to penetrate the collagen that had been injected into her boisterously full lips. She dabbed her mouth dry with a crisp napkin and stood to receive a light kiss on the cheek, reciprocating with a dainty brush of her cheek against mine.

'So how are you?' she enquired earnestly as I sat down opposite her, a little startled to notice a stylishly attired waiter materialise to my left almost immediately.

'I'm good, thanks,' I answered before gesturing towards our serf. 'Are you drinking? Glass of wine maybe?' I ventured, hoping to oil her up a little.

She looked at her glass of mineral water for a second, as if soliciting its opinion on what it thought about having some company on the table.

'Ahm . . . you know what? I will. I'll have a vodka tonic please,' she replied.

I ordered a glass of the first red wine that caught my eye and handed the waiter back the wine menu. The most imperceptible of nods obviating the need for him to actually speak, he took it from me and slunk off towards the bar.

'And how was your meeting? Did it go well?' Rebecca asked.

What meeting? Oh right: The meeting with my prospective agent.

'Hard to tell at this stage really,' I said sagely. 'Curtis Brown is a big operation. So while they have the reach you like to see in an agency, I wouldn't like to kid myself that I'm going to be their number one priority, you know? Don't want to sign up with them and get lost in the crowd. I'm sure that wouldn't happen, they're very professional, but you never know. It's early days at this stage anyway.'

'I see. And what kind of writing is it that you do, exactly?'

No specifics—roll out the stock answer.

'Non-fiction. Quite often it really is stranger than fiction.'

'I see.'

'I'm interested in why people do what they do, you know?'

Her eyebrows arched pensively, as she absorbed the apparent complexity of what I'd just said. No creases—Botox, probably. Unnaturally firm breasts as well: definitely had some work done there. Wouldn't fancy sitting beside her on a flight to Sydney—she'd be liable to pop. Still, it was money well spent: she looked the part all right.

'Right, right. That's so interesting,' she said slowly, like it required some degree of effort.

'Beats working.'

'It certainly does,' Rebecca agreed, the purified reconstituted fibrillar bovine collagen that had been injected into her lips for the purpose of soft tissue augmentation finally conceding defeat and allowing a near-genuine smile break through to the surface, accompanied by a flash of pearly white teeth, the reconstruction and cosmetic enhancement of which could have bought me a 1996 Range Rover Vogue SE with full service history. 'Work with me is an absolute fright at the moment,' she continued, keen to assert her place in the grand scheme of things.

'Really? The property scene still buzzing so, is it?'

'Oh my, yes. Particularly at the top end, which is where we operate mostly. Buying large period homes and reconfiguring them into bespoke apartments, that sort of thing. Very sought after. And people just seem to have the money,' she said incredulously, nearly indignant at the thought of others being able to buy into the lifestyle she was born into.

'It's a great business really. You'll always do well in property if you're in it for the long haul,' I said, scanning the menu quickly as our disconsolately deferential waiter approached.

Rebecca wasn't 'terribly hungry' and just ordered a salad. Not having had my usual fortifying breakfast on account of my early start, I was bloody ravenous, but didn't want to be munching away on a starter with her examining me, so I went for the most substantial looking main course I could find on the all-Italian menu.

As our luncheon progressed, I could tell Rebecca was paying close attention to everything I was saying and doing, sizing me up according to her own, Harpers-&-Queen-endorsed criteria, perhaps wondering if there was any way she could ever envisage introducing me to Tristram and Hermione at Glyndebourne. I suspected my chances were slim, to say the least. Which was perfectly fine by me—I knew from the off that she could never possibly interest me to any degree. She wasn't an unpleasant person by any stretch—if anything, it was quite the opposite: she was far too nice, verging on the boring; painfully well bred and far too reserved to get drunk and have a laugh. What I couldn't figure out was what on earth she was doing as a registered member of DatingDirect.com: surely there was no end of eligible, moneyed bachelors in her circle? What was she doing slumming it with the proletariat? She had, she told me, as she picked elegantly at her salad, met up with quite a few men over the course of her four-month-long membership of the site, but had not yet met 'someone who [she] felt really strongly about'.

'It's funny really when you think about it,' she said staring out the window somewhat blankly, as if talking aloud to herself, 'I never thought I'd ever do anything like *this*, you know?' She waved her hands backwards and forward across the gulf dividing us. 'I always thought that I'd just grow up, get a job, meet a nice boy and get married and have children. Just like my parents, who I always thought had a model marriage. But it hasn't worked out like that. For them, or for me. Especially lately. Every time I go out with a man, I quickly see something in them that I don't like. And yet the people who introduce us tell me we've so much in common and that we're a great match—you know the sort of thing—and then, after a couple of weeks, I just know there's nothing *real* there. And they seem totally baffled by this—amazed that I could reject them.'

My God—there was a cognitive capacity there. Of sorts.

'Maybe you're looking too closely too early,' I ventured, trying to recall some of the 'tough love' guff Dr Phil and the like shamelessly dispense to trailer-park trash every day on national television. I was however, keenly aware that Rebecca was basically telling me that, as our relationship entered its twenty-fifth minute, her early warning system had detected something, perhaps many things, in me that gave her reason to move from DEFCON 5 to DEFCON 3.[3]

'Possibly. But I like to think I've got good instincts,' Rebecca said firmly.

'I'm sure you do,' I said. 'And I think in situations like these it's important to go with your instincts.'

Check please.

'Yes, I think you're absolutely right. So what has you on the singles scene? Any close calls over the years?'

'Oh, you know. A few that at the time felt like they were the real thing, but looking back from where I am now, I don't think they would have worked out in the long term. Of course, had I followed through with one of them, I may very well not be where I am now, if you know what I mean.'

'I do, I do,' Rebecca agreed, allowing herself a knowing smile. 'I don't know if people realise how fundamentally different their life could have been had they stayed in a particular relationship. It's quite a scary thing to consider really . . . best not to dwell on it, I think,' she said. More to herself than to me, I thought, though I agreed with her wholeheartedly.

'Good point. So, any plans for the weekend?' I asked innocuously.

'Another blind date,' she said, rolling her eyes wearily, before checking herself. 'Oh God, that sounded awful, but you know

3. Defense readiness conditions, or DEFCON as they are commonly known, describe progressive alert postures. DEFCONs are graduated to match situations of varying military severity, and are numbered 5,4,3,2, and 1 as appropriate. DEFCONs are phased increases in combat readiness. In general terms, these are descriptions of DEFCONs:

DEFCON 5—Normal peacetime readiness

DEFCON 4—Normal, increased intelligence and strengthened security measures

DEFCON 3—Increase in force readiness above normal readiness

DEFCON 2—Further Increase in force readiness, but less than maximum readiness

DEFCON 1—Maximum force readiness.

what I mean, don't you? Sometimes it does feel like something of a chore—getting yourself all dressed up, friends ringing to wish you well, putting on your 'happy, positive face' and setting forth to meet yet another complete stranger. And then going home wondering why on earth you bothered . . . God, I sound frightful, don't I?'

'No, not really,' I said, more out of empathy than personal experience. 'But why do it so, if it doesn't interest you? Are you happy being single?'

'A lot of the time, yes, I am. But then, like everybody else I suppose, I'd like to have someone special in my life as well. To share my life with someone. But at this stage, I think I'm a little worried that I'll have to share too much! The dreaded compromises that seem inevitable . . .'

'Yeah, there's no getting away from compromise. They say it doesn't feel like compromise, of course, that you don't feel you've conceded ground on a given issue, because you love the person and you're happy to make provision for them and their preferences and all that, but from the outside looking in, I know I've seen a lot people totally subjugate themselves to the whims of their partner.'

'You know what?' Rebecca said, folding her napkin carefully before placing both her outstretched hands on the table. 'We'll have to meet up in a year's time and report on our progress. Or lack of!'

I interpreted her chirpy declaration as a polite suggestion that our time together, though precious and laden with intimacy, was nearly up.

'Agreed. Unless of course, you're happily married and your possessive husband won't condone you fraternising with other men,' I said, taking a last sip of wine before signalling the terminally bored waiter for the check.

'Now that's a compromise too far,' she replied a little cheekily.

Outside, the weather had turned a little nippy. The jacketless Rebecca rubbed her arms vigorously across her scantily clad chest as we said our goodbyes. (I was on the verge of asking her if she needed any help, but thought better of it: despite the fact that I knew I was never going to see her again, I felt I had acquitted myself reasonably well thus far and didn't want to waste a perfectly good quip on someone who I knew wouldn't appreciate it.)

'Well, Donal, it's been a pleasure meeting you. I really enjoyed our lunchtime chat,' she said, setting me up for a soft blow-off. Probably play the geography angle. 'I'm not sure how far either of us commitment-phobes could consider taking anything right now, especially with you in Dublin and me over here, but who knows? We'll keep in touch, shall we?'

'Absolutely,' I said smiling politely, playing along with her. *Commitment-phobes.* In fairness, that was good: not relying on a stock line but instead taking something from the actual exchange to form the basis of your rejection. She certainly was a polished young lady.

'Kiss,' she instructed, once again proffering her soft cheek for me to brush against lightly.

'Take care, Rebecca, it was lovely to meet you. All the best,' I said, and turned to walk in the opposite direction, not quite knowing where I was headed, before turning around once again to give her a cheery wave, letting her know that, with time, my fragile heart would mend and I would able to love again.

She didn't turn around though.

———

I had a couple of hours to kill before my after-work drinkies with Jane so I bought a paper and repaired to a quiet pub for a drink and a toasted sandwich—I was still starving after my light lunch. As it neared four-thirty I figured I'd best make my way towards Covent Garden, just to make sure I had the place sussed out before the time of our meeting. I took a tube to Leicester Square and from there strolled across to Bedford Street to check out the precise location of Bacchanalia. Even though I was far too early, I decided to go in and wait for Jane: I'd been up since all hours and was already quite tired and couldn't face walking around for another hour before showtime. I ordered a drink and commandeered a table affording me an unobstructed view of the door.

Finally, six o'clock rolled around and I started to pay closer attention to the thirsty patrons arriving in to the bar. Apart from the headshot accompanying her profile on the site, Jane had also sent me one other photo of herself, so I had a fair idea of what to expect. As six-thirty approached and what I had a fair idea of what to expect had not materialised, I began to wonder if I had the right bar or not. Her place of work was apparently close by, there was no terrorist incident to report of, my phone was on, she had my number, fashionably late only covers you for twenty minutes or so . . . where the hell was she? I got another drink and picked up my paper again to kill some time. I considered having a go at the crossword, but then decided against it, remembering that they do my head in. Six forty-five announced itself and still no sign of Jane. A tad pissed off at this stage, I sent a terse text message, enquiring casually as to whether or not she was going to bother making an appearance. When I got no reply ten minutes later, I downed the remains of my drink and made for the door.

On my return to Dublin, my stunningly inept service provider informed me that I had four new messages. Two were from Jane: the first I could hardly decipher, riddled as it was all sorts of inter-ference; and the second was her offering some sort of garbled apology for not turning up, claiming that 'something came up' all of a sudden and that she was 'ever so sorry' and hoped that we could arrange to 'do it again sometime'. The third was from the guy behind the speed dating thing, wanting to know if I was inter-ested in attending the next event he was organising. In the message he informed me I had actually received a tick from one of the women in my group. One tick! Probably from the tracksuit-clad 40-year-old and all, knowing my luck. The final message was from Paul, requesting details of the away fixture—I put off filing my report until the next day and headed for home.

14

Oh. My. God.[1]

---

1. Not in a good way.

I'd only myself to blame at the end of the day, I suppose. We were well into August, and after being stood up by Jane in London that week,[2] I figured that the best strategy to adopt was the old get-back-up-on-the-horse one, so I decided to get out there again as quick as I could. Thankfully, there was a fresh 'wink' waiting for me on the Anotherfriend.com site when I checked in the following day. I read the related profile and was delighted to note that the young lady in question, Maria, 29, was of Italian extraction and had been living in Dublin for the past five years, having moved here when she finished university. Her profile was quite witty, and though there was regrettably no photo attached, I sent her a quick message to say hello and what have you. A rather lengthy reply followed quickly thereafter, in which Maria explained that she was not only a new member but also a digital

2. The day after I returned from London Jane sent me a long e-mail, offering an explanation for her no-show. Apparently, as the hour of our proposed rendezvous approached, Jane had become quite nervous at the prospect of meeting me. Turned out she had not been in a relationship of any kind for quite some time, and the last one she was in ended on less-than-favourable terms—she had been living with a law lecturer from her university whom she met whilst completing the final year of her studies, and after two years of what seemed to her to be blissful harmony, he upped and left her to return home to his still-doting wife. Jane, quite understandably, was devastated by this and had rejected all further advances for a year or so until her sister finally persuaded her to give the dating thing another shot. She did, and met some 'quite charming men' but found herself balking at the prospect of taking things too seriously with any of them. And so, last week, when she should have been wrapping up whatever work-related business it was that had been consuming her time for the previous few weeks in preparation for our little assignation, she had a 'panic attack' of some description. Feeling she couldn't face meeting me (not on her own there), she called her sister and they agreed to meet for a drink beforehand. And one drink turned into two, and two turned into three . . . you get the idea. I had naively thought that our correspondence had attained a certain openness, and was quite surprised by this revelation (which took much longer to detail than the abridged version here). Nonetheless, however cruel it may sound, I naturally declined politely when Jane rather cheekily asked if we could make arrangements to meet when I was next in London.

camera-less new member. I gave her the benefit of the doubt and our correspondence continued for most of the day with a flurry of e-mails. The pattern repeated itself the next day, and the day after, with the result that, barely a week into it, Maria was suggesting we meet for lunch in town the following Tuesday. Though ordinarily I avoid meeting anyone on Tuesdays,[3] I made an exception for Maria. She e-mailed me her mobile number, I called her later that night and arrangements were put in place—the Boulevard Café on Exchequer Street at 12.45.

Good result, I thought to myself as I parked the BX in my usual spot near the flats on Golden Lane—a clear case of bouncing back if ever there was. I strolled down to the restaurant with a spring in my step, looking forward to meeting Maria, who, in place of a photo had offered a fairly comprehensive description of herself: 5'8" (a good height), very slim (the 'very' was her own inclusion and quite reassuring), dark skin (always a winner with me), long black hair (she *was* Italian), and *black* eyes (I know—hubba hubba). Furthermore, she told me what she'd be wearing—a black trouser suit with a white blouse. (I know it's considered a staple of the modern working woman's wardrobe, and maybe it's because I don't come into contact with these office-based specimens very often, but there's something about attractive women in black trouser suits that really does it for me, especially when the ensemble is topped off with one of those corporate identity cards swinging from a lanyard that are so common nowadays.)

I was a little early for our meeting so I took a seat at a table by the window, ordered a drink and waited for Maria. 12.50 rolled around and I noticed an elegantly dressed woman in heels striding confidently down the opposite side of the street. Tall, long

3. Tuesday is my official day off, when I take myself into town and catch a movie, buy a book, have a bite to eat, stroll around for a bit, and have a couple of drinks before returning home reinvigorated and ready to resume battle with the world the following day. It's become something of a ritual with me. Kind of like John Goodman's Walter Sobchak character in *The Big Lebowski* and his strict observance of Shomer Shabbos except in reverse: where he did nothing, I do lots. But, like I said, these were extenuating circumstances— couldn't let the fragile Jane hex me in my quest.

black hair, pleasingly tight fitting black trouser suit—this was looking good. She crossed the road without looking—a flagrant breach of the Green Cross Code—had to be Italian. Lovely. In she came, cast her eye around for a minute, saw me at my table pretending to be engrossed in a book, and marched over.

'Donal?' she enquired, elongating the second and last syllable of my name in a slightly husky, and terribly sexy, accent.

I looked up casually from my book and smiled broadly at her for a second before wishing to God I had waited until I had seen a photo of her before acquiescing to our lunch date.

Why? I'll tell you why. Maria was decidedly hirsute. I can handle many shortcomings in a woman's appearance—Lord knows I'm far from a perfect specimen myself—but if there is one thing about a woman's physicality that positively makes me gag, it's unsightly and excessive body hair. Don't get me wrong now— a very fine spread of barely perceptible, peach fuzz-like down on the arms is acceptable, but actual hair, jet black in colour, virtually cascading down in front of the ears before coming to rest in decreasing spirals matted to the cheeks is an absolute no go. (There are harrowing legacy issues as to why this is so.[4])

> 4. After finishing school I took myself off to London for the summer of 1988 in the hope of securing an entry-level position with a stock broker. Unfortunately, the ramifications of the tumultuous events which had occurred the previous October—on Monday 19 October to be precise, when stock markets around the world went into freefall—meant that all the brokers I approached were, quite apart from not hiring any new staff, actually letting many people go, forcing me to seek employment in other fields. And so it was that on Thursday 14 July I found myself attending for interview at the offices of an insurance company in a decidedly dreary industrial complex in North London. At the appointed hour I was ushered into the office for my interview, where I was greeted by a rather dowdy creature called Sharon, somewhat less than resplendent in a grey skirt and jacket that had both seen better days and a peach coloured viscose top with a very generously scooped out neckline which drew more attention to her rather enormous breasts than I felt was appropriate in a workplace setting.
>
> The interview got underway and was going well enough, despite Sharon's overt racism. (When perusing my cv she had a little

'Maria. Hi,' I said weakly, standing to shake her equally hairy paw, sitting down again quickly before I fainted.

Maria sat down, an innocent smile on her face. Poor thing, she had no idea of the effect she was having on me. Lucky for her, my being in town for 12.30 meant I hadn't had my breakfast, because at that point I didn't think I'd have been able to keep it down. She was positively ape-like. It was Darwinian in the extreme.

'Hi. It's very nice to meet you. This is a nice place, isn't it?' she said breezily.

'Yeah, it's fine. I haven't been here in a while though. Do you come here often?' I asked disinterestedly, trying not to look at her too closely.

'Yes, a little bit. With some friends from the office on a Thursday maybe, you know?'

Some friends—you'd think they'd take her aside for a minute and let her in on the reason she was still single.

4. *contd* trouble understanding my Leaving Certificate results, which I had taken the liberty of projecting forward by a couple of months based on how I felt I had performed in the exams—big mistake—but said there was 'another Paddy' working there and she'd get him to 'translate them' for her.) Sharon seemed duped by the enthusiastic attitude I managed to convey and a second-round interview seemed secure. As we were wrapping up, Sharon leaned forward to emphasise some point or other, practically parking her gigantic breasts atop the blot-free leather-encased blotter on her desk. To this day I have no idea what she actually said in those closing minutes, so transfixed was I by the grotesque sight which loomed large in my vision, for sprouting cheekily from the valley of Sharon's cleavage was nothing less than a tuft of hair! I shit you not. I was repulsed and engrossed at the same time, not wanting to look but feeling I had no choice but to continue staring until such time as I could confirm that that was indeed what it was. And so I stared. And stared. Sharon noticed my diverted gaze and looked down at her chest, wondering what could be distracting me. She caught sight of the topiary vying for my attention and immediately straightened up in her chair, adjusting her top quickly so as to conceal the offending foliage. Her face reddened considerably, as did mine, but for different reasons entirely—she was the one at fault. The interview ended in a foggy haze and I made my way outside quickly, sucking in deep breaths of fume-filled not-so-fresh air. Needless to say, I didn't get a second interview.

'Yeah, sure. That's cool.'

Ten minutes into it and I was dying to go home. It was a real shame, too—if you took a shears to her for a half hour or so, Maria would be a cutie and no mistake. The bod was flawless, the hair—on her head—had a lovely silky sheen to it, her skin was indeed a lovely dark tan colour, teeth were perfect and bright white, the black eyes were captivating . . . But the black hair covering her arms and cheeks, and whatever other regions weren't on display, and which I had no desire to discover, was just too much. How could an educated, modern woman let herself go like that? I know the continentals have a much more relaxed attitude to hairy armpits than do ladies here, in the UK and the US, but facial hair on a woman is an absolute no no, wherever you live. And there's no excuse for it—I'm a bloke and even I know all about depilation, epilation, laser treatments, waxing and whatever you're having yourself.

I'll say this for her though; she was blissfully ignorant of her condition. As we ordered our food she continued to chat away gaily, recounting some allegedly hilarious incident in the office the previous day involving a female colleague of hers, a bike messenger and a rather bawdy comment uttered a little too loudly. I missed the end of the story though, as I was trying to pick a spot on the far wall just right of her eyeline to focus on.

'Don't you think that's funny, no?' Maria asked, seeming a little hurt I hadn't laughed on cue.

'Oh, it is, it is,' I said hurriedly, manufacturing a soft giggle. 'Sounds like you have a good time at work.'

'Yes, I like my job a lot. It's very different to other places I have worked in before. Everybody is very nice, we all get along well. We are like a small family, you know? I don't like big companies so much, where people just come to work, do their jobs and go home and you have no interaction with the other people there.'

'I know what you mean,' I said agreeably, though I didn't.

'And so what about you? Do you like your job?' she enquired politely, fixing her lovely eyes on me.

What job?

'Me? Well, I don't see it as a real job, you know? Sometimes I like

it, sometimes I don't,' I said to my chicken, which I was rapidly losing interest in.

'Hello, I'm over here,' Maria said a minute later, waving playfully
at me across the table. 'Donal,' she then said quite firmly, putting
down her fork and pushing her salad forward a little to rest her
arms on the table. 'Is something wrong with you?'

Talk about the pot calling the kettle black.

'Sorry?' I said. 'What do you mean?'

'Well, you are not talking too much and you seem to be in
another place, do you know what I mean? From your e-mails I got
an impression that you were a funny man, very interesting and so
on and so on. And when we spoke on the telephone the other
night you sounded polite and friendly, but now something is
different. What is it? Have I said something I should not have?'

Oh, God. What a nightmare. She was perfect. Well, not perfect,
but great, in so many ways. Ordinarily, I'd be Funtime Frankie,
throwing out gem after gem in an effort to get to see her again in
the hope of some night being able to shag her brains out. But I just
couldn't get over the hair thing. What to say? Anything other than
the truth.

'I'm not sure, Maria. I don't feel very well, to be honest with
you.'

'Oh no? What's the matter?'

Your locks.

'Might have been something I ate last night,' I ventured, rubbing
my stomach tenderly the way a six-year-old would when trying to
skive off school.

'Aye aye, that's not good. Maybe this is not such a good place to
be then, no?' she said helpfully.

'Yeah, I think you're right. I'm very sorry about this, I really am.
I was looking forward to meeting you.'

'Don't be silly. If you are not well, then you are not well. We can
have a lunch another time when you are better.'

I don't think so.

'Yes, I think that's the best idea,' I said gravely, folding my
napkin across my plate to signal my readiness to leave. 'I'll just go
to the bathroom. Back in a minute.'

I got up and gestured to the server to produce the check double quick before making my way to the toilet, where I splashed a bit of water on my face for effect.

'No no no, not at all,' I said to Maria as she tried to give me some money to cover her part of the bill. 'I've ruined your lunchtime, I'm very sorry. It's the least I can do.'

And so it was. I felt really bad about the way things had panned out, particularly because in every respect she was a great catch. Apart from her hirsuteness.

'Well, goodbye. It was nice to meet you, even if it was only for a short time,' Maria said jokingly as we parted company on South Great George's Street. 'I hope you feel better soon.'

'I'm sure I will,' I said, shaking her hand rather formally before hailing a taxi that was careening up the road. 'Bye. And sorry again, Maria.'

'Don't be silly, Donal. You go home and go to bed. Send me an e-mail when you are better and maybe we will talk again, yes?'

'Okay, I'll do that. Bye.'

——

'You're kidding me?' Paul said in disbelief when I told him the story that evening. 'Bit of a pelt on her, yeah? That's gross all right.'

'It's a sickener. Apart from that, she's a honey-in-waiting—great bod, good fun, lovely face. You know . . . were it unblemished, like.'

'So what are you gonna do about it?'

'What can I do? I can hardly look at her. She'll think I'm cross-eyed if I meet her again.'

'Maybe you could bring it up in conversation. Subtly, like, in a very discreet kind of way.'

'Right. How exactly do you propose I tell her she's a bit too furry for my liking?'

'Hang on a sec, I'll ask Rach. This is definitely chick's territory.'

'No, don't ask her! She'll freak. Do you not remember what she was like after the whole Louise episode? She's been shooting me daggers every time I've seen her since.'

'So what have you got to lose? Relax. Rach? Rach?'

'Hello, Donal,' Rachel said a minute later.

'Oh, hi, Rachel, how are you?'

'Fine, thanks. And you?'

'Grand, thanks. How's the little fella?'

'He's brilliant. Paul said you'd something to ask me?'

'Oh, it was nothing really. It doesn't matter.'

'About some Italian girl you met for lunch today?'

'Oh, yeah. Maria. Lovely girl. Really lovely.'

'He's already told me what you said about her, Donal.'

Moron.

'And I have to say, I think you've got some cheek. You're no Brad Pitt yourself, you know?' Rachel continued.

'I know, I know. I was just saying that it's a little off-putting, you know? For me anyway. Apparently, some men think it's quite a turn-on, the whole hippie goddess thing. Loads of websites devoted to it. Apparently.'

'So you want to know how you can bring it up without offending her to the point where she quite rightly tells you she never wants to see you again?'

'Exactly,' I heard Paul affirm in the background.

'Well, kind of, yeah. I know it's not cool maybe; especially so early on and all, and I'm normally very flexible when it comes to this kind of thing, but excessive hair freaks me out, to be honest with you. And with good reason—lost out on a job over it. Did I ever tell you that story? About your one in the insurance company interviewing me? Didn't really want the job, but I had to get something sorted out pretty quick. Anyway, I thought I was through to the second round handy enough, and then she leans forward— the top she had on had a really low neckline, yeah? So she leans forward and I swear to God, I spot this little tuft of hair sprouting out from her . . .'

'My God, you're a complete disaster. I think it'd be very beneficial for you if from time to time you considered things from these girls' perspectives. That's all I'll say. I'll hand you back to Paul, Donal. Bye.'

'What? Oh, right. Yeah. See you Rachel, take care.'

'What did you say to her, you fool?' Paul demanded when he came back on the line. 'She's giving me a right filthy.'

'I didn't say anything to her. I was just telling her about the legacy issues I have with the whole hirsute thing and she went all cool on me.'

'Don't worry about it—post-natal what-have-you. Listen, mate, you should look at this one carefully. Try and get over the hairy thing. She's Italian, you know? *Serie A*, bit of class. Because God knows, you're doing shite domestically, like.'

'Cheers. Always good to talk to you.'

15

I was strolling through Bushy Park the following Friday evening and couldn't get over all the cute chicks out walking their dogs. All I had for company was my iPod, which, effective as it was when it came to blocking out the noise of shrieking children, kind of isolated me from the adult general public. (Which, truth be told, was also why I brought it with me wherever I went.) But this dog thing looked like a good angle, so I thought I'd give it a shot. Where to get a dog though? I didn't want to actually buy one outright in case things didn't work out between us and I'd have to give him one of those 'It's-not-you-it's-me' speeches before leaving him in a shelter. I just wanted one for a couple of days on a trial run so I'd get an idea of what the payoff might be.

Thankfully, fate intervened—threw me a bone if you like. After she had borne him an heir, Paul figured the least he could do was reward Rachel with a weekend away in a spa down the country. Naturally, she was thrilled with this uncharacteristic display of selflessness on his part and jumped at the idea. I offered to look after Ben, their cute little springer spaniel, saving him the expense of boarding the little fella. Paul was cool with the idea—especially after I'd explained to him how I intended to put him to use, walking around the parks and down the pier etc., chatting up cool chicks en route. Rachel wasn't so enthused, however, and only relented after a lengthy interview process and a solemn promise from me to comply fully with all the requirements and procedures she had set down in Ben 2.0 which she had typed up, printed off and inserted in a plastic pocket.

The following week, after dropping them to the airport, I brought García[1] to his new home. He kind of knew me from being over in their place and seemed to settle in well enough. Fond of him and all as I was, I wasn't sure about letting him sleep in the house, even though it was one of the eight 'Ben's Commandments': 'Ben always sleeps indoors. He likes the kitchen, but not too near the fridge.' What was she on? I didn't want him doing his business all over the place, even though Rachel had, somewhat sniffily I might add, declared him fully housetrained when I made enquiries. As a compromise, I set his basket and blankets down in the garage, filled his bowl with water, and bade him a good night.

Upstairs in bed reading my book, I heard a beseeching whine drift through the house. I tried to ignore it, figuring he was just a bit lonesome for his mommy, but he wouldn't give it up. After an hour I caved in and went downstairs to let him in, rearranging his accoutrements in front of the oven, while he padded around beside me, inspecting his new quarters. He seemed to approve and settled down quick enough. I returned to my bed and resumed my reading, only to be discommoded once again not ten minutes later by more banshee-like wails from the kitchen. Downstairs again and there he was, trying to scratch his way through the door in a bid to locate me. Once he saw me he calmed down immediately, slipped into dreamy docile mode and curled up at my feet as I sat at the table having a smoke (flagrantly ignoring Commandment

1. On the way back from the airport, Ben dozing contentedly on the passenger seat beside me, I decided on a name change: Ben just wasn't going to cut it out there with the ladies—I needed something with a bit more pzazz, a bit of zing. An unforgettable name, which would I hoped, help attractive women out walking their own dogs to remember my name, even if it was only by association. Looking at his silky, chocolate coat and noble features, I settled on García, a name which I thought reflected his proud Spanish heritage infinitely better than the more pedestrian 'Ben'.

Number Seven in the operating manual—'You wouldn't smoke in front of a child, so please don't smoke in front of Ben—passive smoking affects dogs too.') Then, I tried reassuring García that I wasn't in fact abandoning him, merely going to bed and that I would see him in the morning, which was by now fast approaching, but he wasn't having any of it: as soon as I closed the door and went upstairs, he was off, crying like a baby. There was nothing for it but to relocate his basket and blankets upstairs to the landing outside my bedroom. His furiously wagging tail indicated his approval and I finally managed to get some sleep, only to wake up the next morning to find him standing completely still not six inches from my bed, staring at me intently, lest I try to disappear on him again.

Shadowing me closely as I prepared my breakfast, García seemed perfectly content once he could see me at all times. He reminded me a lot of a girl I went out a couple of years ago—cute, warm and friendly, but always enquiring after my movements, and in need of a level of RDA[2] beyond that which I felt was necessary. He munched away on his dog food for a bit but then turned his nose up at it and came sniffing around me once again, looking for a bit of table-top action. Breaking yet another Benmandment, I gave him a piece of my waffle. He seemed to like the carbs well enough, but I figured he was angling for a taste of the good stuff, so I tossed him the fatty rind from my rashers, which I always discard anyway. He was loving me now all right, jumping up and down, tail going like mad. Capitalising on his good mood, I let him out the back for a few minutes so he could mark his territory, and then decided we'd better hit the park and see what was happening.

Down the hill by the lake there was an elderly woman feeding the ducks. As I strolled past her, headed for the outer path along by the Dodder River, she caught sight of García and started mooning all over him. I stopped politely to let her molest him for a bit.

'Aren't you gorgeous? Yes, you are. Yes, you are,' she said cooingly, as if she were addressing her grandson. 'What's the little fella's name?' she asked, looking up at me.

'García,' I replied, knowing it would be wasted on her.

2. Required Daily Affection.

'Sorry?'

'García,' I repeated. 'It's Spanish.'

C'mon lady, wrap it up, I've got bigger fish to fry here.

'I know it's Spanish,' she said quickly. 'It's just that it says 'Ben' here on his name tag.'

Shit. Forgot about that.

'Yeah, well he *was* called Ben originally, but I'm thinking García suits him better now, you know?' I said, pulling gently on the leash, trying to get him away from her. He wasn't cooperating though, whore for affection that he was.

'Well, it seems very strange to change a dog's name. They get used to it and respond to it . . .'

'Maybe. We'll see. C'mon boy, let's go,' I said, keen to get off. 'García. C'mon, boy.'

'He seems quite happy here, don't you, little fella?' she said, rubbing his ears in an inappropriate fashion. The little slut was loving it, of course.

'What's that?' she said, as if she'd missed something he'd said to her. 'You want some bread, do you?'

'I'd rather you didn't give him any of that,' I said, perhaps a little testily, but I just wanted shut of her. She looked up sharply at me.

'I'm trying to cut down on his carbs,' I said, smiling weakly. Lost on her. Could have done with losing a few pounds herself and all. 'García. Come on, let's go.'

Wouldn't budge.

'Are you sure this is your dog?'

'What? Of course it's my dog. C'mon García, good boy. Let's go, good boy.'

Finally, the little bugger deigned to pay some heed to my bidding and got into step behind me.

'Well, best be going. Bye,' I said politely, turning to head for home before Miss Marple got it into her head to ring the ISPCA.

So day one was a dead loss. That night García stood watch over my bed once again. I had by now grown accustomed to his beady brown eyes tracking my every move, and whilst it was gratifying to have for company a creature whose needs were so rudimentary— food, shelter and affection—I wasn't so sure that it would suit me on a long-term basis. It was a real commitment, taking on a pet, and while there were rewards, of sorts, in terms of loyalty and unwavering devotion—attributes hard enough to find in most people—it was a lot of work. My situation was not unlike that of a single parent, I thought to myself the following morning as I reluctantly spread some old newspapers over a puddle of his making in the kitchen.

After breakfast I made a few calls to catch up with some friends, hoping to arrange for a few home-cooked dinners to be handed up to me the following week. News of my dog-sitting was greeted with a mixture of surprise and disbelief. I explained the ulterior motives inherent in my selfless act, only to be met with snorts of derision. A tad miffed at their lack of support for my endeavours, I confirmed housecalls for Tuesday and Thursday and then checked my e-mail[3] as García took up position under the table—

3. I'm delighted to report that, as predicted, my appeal to women resident in the Baltic States showed no sign of abating. One of the messages in the inbox was from the rather-delicious-looking Tatyana, 27, originally from Vitebsk, which is in the north-eastern part of Belarus, on the Western Dvina River, northeast of Minsk.

First mentioned in 1021, Vitebsk was engaged in something of a pass-the-parcel game, passing first to Lithuania in the 14th century, then to Poland in the 16th century, and finally to Russia in the 18th century, 1772 to be exact. The city of Vitebsk currently has a population of some 345,000 people, and is a prominent river port and railroad intersection lying in a predominantly agricultural region. Manufacturing activity is concentrated on the production of machine tools, electrical instruments, processed food, textiles, and building materials. (I'm on top of things, and no mistake.) The bright lights of Minsk proved irresistible to Tatyana, however, and she moved there to complete her studies in accountancy. She still lives there now, and works for a large chain of bakeries, counting all their dough. (I kill myself.)

Tatyana opened the lines of communication with this:

Hi Donal,
I saw your profile and I am interested in knowing you. I was introduced here by a friend who got her husband from this site and they both live in London. Actually, I cannot say I am looking for a husband now but I am looking for someone I can spend this

draped across my shoes so I couldn't move without him know-ing—and drifted off for a snooze. An hour or so later, I was in the mood for *The Guardian*, as I usually am on a Saturday, and after placating García with a chewy treat, I attempted to leave the house. Not a chance: he was at the door before me, leaping ever higher at the thoughts of some fresh air, bounding across open meadows in search of mischief. Or a shag, maybe. So I strolled up to the shops with him and tied him to a bollard outside, in much the same way as a cowboy would his trusty steed before entering the saloon for a brawl. When I returned, there were no less than four small children making a scene with him, shrieking with delight as he licked their fawning hands, his tail beating like a metronome on 240 bpm. All very well, he was a gorgeous looking creature, but this wasn't the sort of action I was hoping for.

Then I remembered that Killiney Hill was a popular spot for canine recreation and decided to trek out there for the crack, stop-ping off en route at a hardware store to buy a cool, chunky metal 'G' key ring, which I switched with the potentially damning 'Ben' tag. (He seemed to like the bit of bling.) We weren't two minutes out of the car when I spotted a woman playing fetch with her honey-coloured Labrador. This was more like it—could get a bit of doggie tennis going on here. A little anxiously, I let my wing-man off his lead, hoping he wouldn't make a bolt for freedom. Fair play to him, he bounded across the grass and started barking

3. *contd summer with, to see how to build a relationship that can be serious. I hope you are lonely too and will like to meet someone with some similar dreams as yours. Please if you will be interested to know more and to see my pics, contact me at ————— @yahoo.com I will be very happy to read from you and to know more about you.*

Adorable really, aren't they? I sent Tatyana an encouraging reply, asking her casually where she was headed on her travels this sum-mer. If she was anything like Vera, she'd reply with a request for me to wire €800 to the local Western Union in Minsk, at which point I'd know what kind of game she was playing. She was very attractive though, I have to say. The photo she had uploaded to the site showed her in an elegant evening dress, looking quite the belle of the ball.

excitedly at the Labrador, who responded in a good-natured way and started gnawing playfully at García. Great life they have, I thought to myself—see a mate, and off they go, straight in for a fumble. If only it were that easy for us bipeds.

'Easy, Lucy. Easy girl,' the dog's owner cautioned as she tramped across the grass towards the cavorting pair.

I opened with 'Hi, there,' as you do. 'Lovely dog. How old is she?'

'She's three,' the woman replied, drawing level with the exhibitionists. Quite attractive she was, too. About my age, I'd say. Long blonde hair tied up in a ponytail. Bright, cheery face, cheeks rosy red from the crisp, fresh air. Sparkling blue eyes. Going for the *Horse and Hound* look—outfitted in green wellies, jeans, quilted Barbour jacket and bright scarf tied loosely around her slender neck.

'How about yours? A boy is it?'

'Yeah, that's right. García,' I said.

'García? Wow, now there's a name,' she said approvingly, bending down to feed his affection habit. 'Isn't it, huh? Aren't you the cool dude, García?'

At last—someone who got the inherent coolness of the name. And could pronounce it properly too. I wasn't sure how these doggie-induced exchanges played out, so I reckoned an easy Starter for Ten was the best option.

'Great day, isn't it?' I said, even though it was actually quite nippy on the exposed hillside overlooking the bay.

'Yes, it is. Though it's nearly always a bit nippy up here on the hill,' she replied pleasantly.

'This a regular spot for you so, is it?' I ventured gamely, bending down to give her dog a bit of TLC.

'Every day nearly, it's great to be able to let her off the leash and hare around for an hour or so.'

'Yeah, it is. Really tires them out.'

This was going well.

'Mummy, mummy.'

Damn it—she's married. Hardly surprising, I acknowledged, as she bent over to greet her little angel, her jacket riding nicely up over her jeans to reveal a lovely, pert behind, which I tried not to look at too obviously as a man, her husband presumably, approached with another toddler slung under his arm like a sleeping bag.

'Hi, there,' I said innocently as he set the little boy down, who proceeded to gingerly stroke García, moving gradually closer as he realised that the chances of him losing a limb were negligible.

'Hello,' he responded a little curtly. 'Are you right?' he said, addressing his wife. 'We'd better be going.'

'Oh? What time is it?' she asked, obviously disappointed she couldn't stay and chat longer.

'After three.'

'Gosh, I didn't think it was that late,' she said, securing the lead to Lucy, and giving García one last rub on the ears.

'Nice meeting you, all the best. And take good care of that beautiful dog,' she said warmly, smiling as she turned to leave.

'I will, don't worry. Bye,' I said.

'Not to worry boy, you weren't to know she was married to that knob,' I said encouragingly to García, picking up the stick discarded by Lucy's owner and throwing it across the meadow for him to sprint after.

'Okay boy, last day. You know what you have to do,' I said softly to García as I opened the car door for him the following afternoon. He bounded in and started scampering around impatiently, a little disappointed with the confined space of the interior of my car. I drove up to Marlay Park, reckoning it would be busy enough on a Sunday.

As I walked across the stone bridge I spotted a likely prospect— an attractive-looking woman in a cheeky pink velour tracksuit, marching along purposefully with, it has to be said, a rather pathetic looking yoke—a terrier of some description. Still, it was the owner and not the dog that I was interested in so I thought I'd give it a lash. Seizing his opportunity to shine, García made straight for her little mutt, circling him playfully, and dragging me into the action as I was attached to the other end of the lead.

'Hi, how's it going?' I said cheerily, hoping for a fulsome reciprocation from my fellow dog-lover.

'Ricky, Ricky, stop. Good boy. Stop it Ricky,' she said to her charge. 'Sorry about that, he's a bit excitable.'

'Aren't they all,' I said knowingly, restraining García as he attempted to mount the mangy-looking tyke.

'Gorgeous dog. What's its name?' she enquired.

'García.'

'Garcia? That's, unusual . . . He's got a beautiful coat though.'

It's Garc*í*a actually, not Garcia. And what's with the, 'though'?

'Well, I'd better be going. Bye. C'mon Ricky, c'mon boy.'

And off she went, doing her power walk, Ricky cantering along beside her.

'Don't worry boy, it wouldn't have worked out anyway—she wasn't feeling it. See how she didn't even get the García thing? Loser.'

He nodded in agreement and we continued gamely on our way, hampered as we were by any number of kids scampering over to pet García. I got a few words in with a couple of cool enough chicks as we strolled up the long path alongside the cricket pitch, but nothing that looked like it was going to lead to an exchange of numbers, so we called it a day and headed back to the house.

'Now listen, boy,' I said sternly to him, dangling a chewy treat tantalisingly in front of him. 'I'm going out for a couple of hours to meet a young lady . . . well, she's not that young, but still—and you can't come. You know I wish you could, but you can't, and that's that, so I want no grief when I'm leaving, okay?'

Oblivious to my plea, he snapped the treat from my hands and scarpered underneath the table to devour the infuriatingly rubbery twig. I seized my opportunity and made for the door, pretending not to hear his simpering whine as he realised the extent of the treachery I had committed against him.

I'd arranged to meet Annette[4] outside The Portobello pub in Rathmines. Not my choice of hostelry, I must stress—I hadn't

4. Annette had boldly added me to her list of 'favourites' on the DatingDirect site, so I took the initiative and sent her a message. That was sometime in July, and we exchanged e-mails a couple of times a week. Bonafides thus established, I bit the bullet a few weeks later and suggested we meet up. She agreed, but rebuffed my initial suggestion for our date: I had an invite to a gallery opening in town on the Thursday and thought it would be a cool thing to swing to for an hour or so—enjoy some complimentary and inoffensive wine, critique the work on show—and then, all going well, scoot off

darkened its door since my college days—and would happily have continued in that vein forevermore, but Annette, a 41-year-old English woman recently arrived in Dublin after a three-month stint in München, didn't know her way around just yet and had suggested we meet there as it was near her apartment.

As I stood outside the pub, bemoaning the decidedly slovenly clientele scuttling in for pints, I found myself actually wondering if García was okay back in the house. Annette trotted up only a few minutes late, and after exchanging pleasantries, I held the door open for her and we went inside. Taking advantage of the view, I checked her out quickly to see what was on offer. She was well preserved for her age, it had to be said, with shoulder-length dyed blonde hair and pleasant enough features. Style-wise she had opted for cork-soled wedges, indigo jeans (one size smaller than I would have recommended, to be honest), and a floral-print wraparound blouse over a tight white vest.

I found a table as far away from the general populace as I could, asked her what she'd like to drink and made for the bar. On my return, she poured the full contents of the small bottle of white wine requested into her glass and took a long, generous gulp, quickly belying her outward nonchalance. After five minutes I knew I wanted to leave and never see her again, and I reckon she probably felt the same way. There was no chemistry between us whatsoever, and we had very little in common; even our *reasons* for holding the same opinions on the most banal of matters differed considerably.

Her glass was drained before I had finished my bottle of beer, but I made no offer of another. As far as I was concerned, we could call it a day, or a night, right now, and no harm done. If she wanted another drink, she could buy it herself, along with one for me.

'Will you have another?' she enquired, clearly more out of manners than enthusiasm.

4. *contd* somewhere for a bit to eat. Suave, no? That's what I thought, but she wasn't having it: she actually said she 'didn't like art'. 'At all'. Not holding out much hope for us hitting it off, I nonetheless happily agreed when she parried with the drinks thing. After all, she was 41, never married, new in town, no close friends to speak of ... could be looking for a bit of company.

'Yeah, go on so. Thanks,' I replied casually.

As soon as her back was turned I whipped out my phone, retrieved the emergency text message I had stored in my outbox, and sent it to Paul, alerting him to my peril. Annette returned and we made another stab at connecting: No use, there was nothing there. For example, she was working in Dublin on contract, and when I asked her what she liked to do in her downtime, she said nothing. As in 'nothing': she liked to lie on the sofa and watch TV.[5] No wonder she was 41 and still single—there appeared to be very little in life that seemed to either interest or excite her. In all fairness I was making all the running, plying her with innocuous questions about her work experience, places she'd lived, her family, friends . . . the whole nine yards, throwing in a bit about myself along the way. But I wasn't in biographer mode the way I usually am with women I'm getting to know—I was merely filling the void between us with aimless banter so we wouldn't be sitting there in complete silence, looking to all the world like a pair of wizened old fogies who'd been married for forty years and were all talked out.

Wondering how best to wrap things up, I disinterestedly asked her what kind of week she had ahead of her.

'Manic. Absolutely manic,' she said, raising her eyes heavenward. 'In fact, I'd better be going soon, I've an early start in the morning.'

Bingo.

'No problem. I'm ready when you are,' I said cheerily, downing the remains of my beer in one and reaching for my jacket.

'Well, listen, it was great to meet you at last, and I hope Dublin is good to you,' I said smiling, the tone of finality discernible in my voice to all but the deaf.

5. I know I have extolled the many and pleasurable virtues of doing nothing on previous occasions, but the kind of nothing Annette liked to do—watching TV all night—amounted to, well, nothing at all really. To the extent that it was almost nihilistic, which is a million miles away from my kind of nothing: I don't even have a basic television subscription anymore—my NTL subscription expired when I was in France and I didn't bother renewing it. Like I said, it's a many-levelled pursuit.

'It was nice to meet you too, Donal,' she said professionally, taking my outstretched hand and proffering one cheek.

I gave her a quick peck and smiled as warmly as the circumstances would permit, and then walked away, turning once to wave politely. I was headed in the opposite direction to my house, but going the right way would have meant both of us enduring another few minutes of awkward smalltalk. Besides, I needed a drink, so I headed down to Cassidy's, ringing Paul on the way to tell him to cancel the emergency phone call.

16

I had begun to feel like one of the code-breakers working at Bletchley Park during World War II as they tried to crack the German Enigma cipher. So many of the women on these online dating sites appeared to be either very reluctant to divulge even the most basic of details about themselves or only too happy to divulge all the wrong ones, that you would wonder how serious they were about actually trying to meet somebody.

When you register as a new member on Anotherfriend.com for instance, you have to fill in a profile of yourself, answering a variety of questions laid out in standard template. This template could be likened to having your own, digital, shop window: it's in your best interests to dress it up as attractively as you can in order to lure punters inside to check out the merchandise. Agreed? Okay. So get this. There is the option to insert, 'Ask me later' or, 'I'll tell you later' as an answer to certain questions: the kind that you may feel more comfortable answering only after a certain level of familiarity or even intimacy, has been attained with someone. Which is fair enough, if the question is about your salary maybe, but not for innocuous questions about what you're into, for example.

I actually came across one woman recently who had selected, 'Ask me later' or, 'I'll tell you later' in eleven different sections of her profile. She wouldn't even reveal what kind of bloody car she drove! How pathetic is that? Did she not she realise the irony inherent in adopting such a clandestine approach, in that no man in his right mind would bother getting in touch with her without at least some basic biographical and personal information, so she would not have the opportunity to tell anybody anything 'later'.

Nearly as bad as not giving enough information are the profiles where someone gives all the wrong information. You nearly feel like getting in touch with them just to tell them that they haven't a hope in hell of meeting anybody with the kind of profile they have posted. Take this one for example:

About Her	
Username:	musicalfeminist [Standard Member]
Last Logged On:	Today
Gender:	Female
Height:	5' 3
Age:	27
Weight:	Not Specified Lbs
Body Type:	Voluptuous
Hair Colour:	Other
Eye Colour:	Hazel
Ethnic Group:	I'll tell you later
Religion:	I'll tell you later
Location:	Dublin, Ireland
I grew up in:	Dublin, Carlow and Cork
I would describe myself as:	I'm a human rights actavist, currently trying to write a thesis. Lover of music, both performing and appreciating.
Marital Status:	Single
I drive a:	
Children:	None
Friends:	Have a few friends
Star Sign:	Sagittarius
Humor:	I enjoy a good joke
Smoking:	Non-Smoker
Emotion:	Ask me later
Drinking:	Socially

Risks:	I take some risks
Favourite Pub:	Which ever 1 I'm in . . .
Physical:	Active
Favourite Band:	I have many . . .
Spending:	I spend enough to enjoy life
Last CD Bought:	
Stress:	I get stressed at times
Occupation:	
Relationships:	Had 2 serious relationships
Income:	Ask me later
Talk Level:	Love to Talk to anyone
Education:	Master's
Relationship Type:	A Date
My ideal partner would be:	Intelligent, fit, egalitarian, enjoys life, enjoys debating issues, someone who loves sharing food with friends . . .
My ideal date would be:	Surprise me . . . I'll try anything once!

A few points, if I may. Her user name for starters—Musical Feminist. Talk about falling at the first fence. How many men would see that and think to themselves, 'Oh yeah, she sounds like a lot of fun'? Not many, if any. Then she refuses to specify her weight, only to describe her body type as 'voluptuous', which with a height of 5'3" could reasonably be interpreted as fat, basically. Which is fine. If you're fat, you're fat. Either get used to it and be happy, or go to a gym and change it. Bit of a rolling stone too, is our musical feminist, having grown up in Dublin, Carlow and Cork. The last two are a bit unfortunate all right, but maybe her parents were a double act in a travelling circus and there was nothing she could about it.

For some bizarre reason, she is reluctant to divulge either her ethnic origins or her religious orientation. Slowly but surely, this great nation of ours is lurching unsteadily towards racial and ethnic pluralism, but I think it's safe to say that, at twenty-seven years of age, our rolling stone is most likely a common or garden Mick, like most of the rest of us. So what's the big deal? She goes on to describe herself as a human rights 'actavist' (which I'm assuming is the same thing as a human rights activist). Again,

maybe it's just me, but I can't see a whole lot of men being mag-
netically attracted to a person who sees this as the defining element of their personality. Apart from a fellow vegan G8 protester,
possibly. She has actually selected her star sign—you are given the,
'I don't believe in it' option—which would suggest that she
accredits such hogwash with some import: scary stuff indeed.

A self-professed music lover, 'both performing and appreciat-
ing', she can't be arsed to list the last CD she bought, which in itself
can sometimes be pretty useful information. I mean, would you
seriously consider getting in touch with someone who actually
admitted to buying one of The Corrs' CDs? Thought not. She
doesn't drive, which means you'd have to be giving her lifts all over
to the place to cello classes and Amnesty International rallies. She
drinks only socially, which could be taken to mean she doesn't get
out a whole lot, and probably explains why her favourite pub is,
'Whatever 1 [she's] in'. Rather cheekily I think, for one who
describes herself as voluptuous, she desires her mate to be 'fit',
amongst other things. And finally, when asked to describe her
ideal date, she plumps for the rather ambiguous, 'Surprise me—
I'll try anything once!', which could be taken the wrong way by
some of the more Neanderthal males scouring the site. I'd say she's
beating them away with a stick. A really big stick.

By way of stark contrast, here's the one I came up with:

Username:	Narky [Premium Member]
Last Logged On:	Today
Gender:	Male
Height:	5'10
Age:	35
Weight:	174 Lbs
Body Type:	Average weight
Hair Colour:	Brown
Eye Colour:	Green
Ethnic Group:	White/Caucasian
Religion:	Catholic
Location:	Dublin, Ireland
I Grew up in:	Dublin

I would describe myself as:	Single, not embarrassing to be seen with in public. No interest in index-linked pensions, tracker mortgages or kids. Greatest achievement to date is not having worn a tie in ten years. Hate working, like drinking, smoking, having a laugh, especially on a Tuesday afternoon when the rest of the world is sitting at a desk.
Marital Status:	Single
I drive a:	Piece of shit
Children:	None
Friends:	Have a few friends
Star Sign:	I don't believe in it
Humor:	I can be sarcastic at times
Smoking:	Occasionally
Emotion:	I am cool and calm
Drinking:	Frequently
Risks:	I live on the edge
Favourite Pub:	An empty one
Physical:	Select activities
Favourite Band:	
Spending:	I spend enough to enjoy life
Last CD Bought:	doves
Stress:	I am calm as a cucumber
Occupation:	Don't have one
Relationships:	Had 2 serious relationships
Income:	€35,000—€50,000
Talk Level:	Talkative with people I know
Education:	Bachelor's
Relationship Type:	A Date
My ideal partner would be:	A smart, witty, cute woman who works to live, likes to travel, hates kids, cooking and gardening. A sense of humour is essential.
My ideal date would be:	See a good movie, preferably in the Screen, a bit of food in The Market bar, and a few beers somewhere you can smoke. Share a taxi home, have a snog and make plans to do it all again.

A clear case of wysiwig if ever there was one, separating the wheat from the chaff from the off. Only someone who is *interested* in the kind of acerbic, confident, independent, intelligent, witty—I could go on, but you get the idea—kind of male that I represent would respond to my profile. And such women would generally fall into one of three categories:

The first would be someone who is like that themselves, and who is secure enough to able to accommodate someone of a similar calibre and nature. Conclusion: happy days—bring it on. The second would be someone who is maybe not quite as urbane and evolved as myself, but who would appreciate these qualities in an opposite number, reckoning, quite justifiably, that some of my unquestionably attractive qualities might rub off on them in time, thereby elevating them to a similar plane of consciousness. Conclusion: perfectly understandable—let's do it. And then there would be that class of foolish woman who, for whatever reason, sets her sights on a man, realises that there is a lot there that is not to her liking, but feels that she is such a sufficiently attractive proposition herself that the man in question—me—would willingly allow her to chip away relentlessly at his person until she has reduced him to a shadow of his former self.[1] Conclusion: keep the hell away from me.

Needless to say, I've had opening gambits in my inbox from many category-three women, whom I dispatched with all good haste and no equivocation, a few from category-two women, whom I replied to in a manner befitting their aspirations, and regrettably few from category-one women, principally because there are so few of them out there, I think.

As I have said before, the major area of concern for me, particularly in relation to the Irish sites, is the reluctance with which most people post a photo of themselves on their profile page. I

1. Don't pretend it doesn't happen. It does. We've all seen it. Whatever goes on behind closed doors is one thing, but the classic public display of this atrocious and frankly pathetic subjugation, to my mind at any rate, is when you see a woman choose a man's clothes for him. While he is standing beside her. In a man's clothes shop. With other people—real men—looking on, a mixture of disgust and pity etched on their faces.

know some of you will think me shallow for harping on about it again, but this is really beginning to bug me. I have a photo up on the site for all to see, and I couldn't care less what people think of it. That's me; get used to it. When I first started out on this online dating lark, if I came across a profile of a woman who sounded interesting but had no photo uploaded, I generally ignored it and forged ahead, scrutinising only profiles with photos attached.[2] In a situation where a woman with no photo uploaded got in touch with me first—as quite a few did, thanks not only to my witty wordsmithing but also because I had a photo uploaded, which at least gave them something to go on and reassured them I didn't look like the back of a bus—I courteously replied to their opening gambit, graciously giving them points for at least taking the initiative. All going well, I would, after say five or six e-mails, hope they would forward a photo to me. (Photos themselves can be deceptive of course, a fact I can readily attest to. The art of photographing oneself to one's best advantage is also something many women seem well versed in. The photos I am always a little suspicious of are the ones where the subject's right or left arm is

2. A definite exception here was Tatyana, who sent me numerous photos of herself with commendable regularity. Furthermore, I was pleased to note a consistent theme in them, in that each shot showed Tatyana wearing less clothes than in the previous photograph. As I said before, in the first one she was wearing a long evening gown. In the second one she was in a short skirt and blouse, sitting at her desk in her place of work. The following week I was treated to a couple of snaps of her in Belarus on her summer holidays, which showed her sitting astride a large stone lion outside a stately home of some note, dressed in a pair of super tight white shorts and matching crop top. Finally, a couple of days later, I received a photo of Tatyana posing playfully on the beach in a skimpy red bikini, allowing me to fully map the contours of her upper torso, the hills and valleys of which I would dearly like to get lost in for a week or two. (Naturally, Paul had instructed me to forward each photo on to him the minute I received it, even going so far as to suggest that I cc him with all our correspondence so he could monitor our progress 'from the sidelines'. I agreed to the photo sharing, but not the cc suggestion—I would have put money on him getting in touch with Tatyana to try and move things along.

raised and to the fore of the shot, in that it suggests the subject took the photo themselves, and more than likely spent about six hours readying themselves for their close-up. It's also probably indicative of a lack of familiarity with technological apparatuses, as most digital cameras these days come equipped with a self-timer, thus obviating the need for such acrobatics. Extrapolating on from this suggests that the lady in question is also probably a hopeless driver, a shortcoming which would test the most solid of relationships.) If and when the photo was finally received and the physicality contained therein was not to my liking I would scale down the frequency and tone of the communications until such time as they realised that I didn't fancy them, saving me the trouble of having actually to say it to them myself, which is some-thing I naturally tried to avoid at all costs, given the potential recriminations such an indelicate communiqué could bring forth. (The trouble I could have saved myself with Maria!)

And so to help decode some of these profiles, I have resorted to some slightly unorthodox measures. Take a situation where I come across an interesting sounding profile, which though not accom-panied by a photo of its author, does contain other information pertaining to their physicality, namely their height and weight. In such cases, I input the relevant stats into a calculator I discovered on the VHI Healthcare website. The Body Mass Index (BMI), calculator tells me if the proposed target of my affections is at a healthy weight for her height. For example, when checking out a few newcomers' profiles on DatingDirect.com I came across one that sounded promising. No photo, but the youngish lady had at least deigned to reveal her height and weight: 5'7" and 140 lbs respectively. So I inputted the data as required. Two seconds later, I learned that Amelia had a BMI of 21.9, putting her comfortably in the normal category (18.5–25). Collating this satisfactory infor-mation with other relevant info supplied, namely hair colour and length, eye colour, age and ethnic grouping, I then began to construct a 3D image of Amelia in my mind. As her physicality took shape, literally, I then strengthened the emerging image by cross-referencing it against women with similar characteristics whom I had actually met, to see if it stacked up in an ultimately pleasing manner. Impressive, no? (A couple of months more of this crack and I could be a profiler for the FBI.) Happily, Amelia made the grade and a cheery introductory message was dispatched.[3]

It's not just the physical side of things that presents problems though when you're analysing profiles. Once you get that bit out of the way, all going well, the next step of the visualisation process involves a preliminary assessment of the person's personality, insofar as that's possible. Make no mistake, whatever about the area of aesthetics, if ever one needs to tread carefully before firing off an opening salvo, it's here, so open to varied interpretation are the words people use to describe themselves.

Using the delightful Amelia as an example once again, here is what she said when describing herself: '*impatient, too sensitive, too smart for my own good, sometimes weird sense of humour, talk too much and write too much, inquisitive, demanding, honest, not shallow, sometimes restless, definitely never bored, kind of private though . . . and you have to work hard to discover more . . .*'. Certainly, there are many ways to decode this particular self-description, both positively and negatively, but it was definitely intriguing. At least Amelia put a bit of thought into its composition, which is more than I can say for most of the women using these sites, who seem to rely on some *Cosmopolitan-Glamour-Company*-endorsed, generic, vague and vacuous vocabulary when called upon to elucidate on what makes them tick.

The descriptions I can least abide are the ones that begin with, 'Well, my friends say I'm . . .' Using this thinly veiled mechanism to come over all modest while at the same time basically saying that you're perfect does my head in. The wordpower of many of these females leaves a lot to be desired as well—the majority of them seem to rely on the same few words and phrases to describe themselves. 'Easy-going'. 'Laid-back'. 'Up for a laugh'. 'Independent'.[4] 'Bubbly'. (Quite often a euphemism for fat—needs to be stringently cross-checked with available height and weight stats. Ditto

3. Call me shallow, fickle, whatever you like, but, put simply, I don't see why I should have to shag anyone who's any fatter than I am.

4. It's truly amazing how many people spell this as, 'independant': Grounds for dismissal from the off.

for cuddly.) And 'attractive', of course. Everyone's attractive, apparently. The most commonly used one though has to be the old 'the rest, you'll just have to find out . . .', which essentially means they couldn't be arsed thinking of anything else to say about themselves, and not that there lie within them untold seams of diversity, waiting to be mined for all their worth by the right man. Just by the by, while I'm at it, I cannot for the life of me figure out why some women insist on describing themselves in the third person, like they're royalty or something. 'Likes to walk'. 'Loves swimming'. 'Enjoys eating out with friends'. Who do they think they are? It's not easy, this crack. It's not easy.

17

At last! A category one woman. One Ellen O'Connell. To save you flicking back a few pages to recap on what constitutes such a specimen, allow me to remind you: a category one woman is basically a female version of me. Though the very idea of such a creature actually existing may fill some of you with equal parts dread and disbelief, I naturally welcomed it with open arms and great enthusiasm. That I had to fly to New York to meet her is neither here nor there at the end of the day.[1] Suffice to say

1. Ellen, 33, a Midlands native happily resident in the Big Apple for the previous four years, where she had forged a successful career for herself in the cut-and-thrust, male-dominated world of high finance on Wall Street, had sent me a 'wink' via the anotherfirend.com site in the early days of my membership. I checked out her profile and, suitably impressed, deigned the situation worthy of further investigation. I responded with a snappy introductory mail, which was well received and answered with one of a similar calibre. From there, our virtual relationship developed quickly both in terms of frequency and format. By frequency I mean that our e-mail exchange went from about thrice weekly to almost daily, and by format I mean that we went from exchanging e-mails via the dating site to exchanging them via our own personal e-mail accounts. Photos of our respective selves were dispatched, at which point I thought I might never

that as the 'Fall' introduced itself, I found myself on the corner of 69th and York on Manhattan's Upper East Side, looking for her apartment building. (She was expecting me, I hasten to add.)

The lift, sorry, elevator, took me swiftly to the 34th floor. I exited to find the door to her apartment handily positioned right in front of me. I knocked and waited, thinking it best not to dwell too long on what I was actually doing. The door opened and there she was in the flesh, pretty much as I had imagined her after much scrutiny of the photos she had sent me (which I had had digitally enhanced and enlarged at great expense). Given the level of intimacy achieved between us thus far, albeit on a purely verbal plane, a hug felt more appropriate than a merely perfunctory and altogether-too-formal handshake. So I hugged her. And it was good.

A friend of hers was there as well—Amy, a very cool chick indeed. She was an art teacher in elementary school in a tough part of Brooklyn. We three chatted away happily for an hour or so and then, satisfied that I didn't represent an immediate threat to Ellen's personal safety, Amy tactfully bade us her leave and left us alone. It was a bright and crisp October day in the city, but not too cold, so we prepared a couple of drinks and moved out to her balcony, where I could smoke and admire the view her lofty perch afforded over the sprawling metropolis: the Time Warner towers to my left near one of *Il Duce*, Mr Trump's, gaudy monuments to vanity, and the leafy canopy of the trees in Central Park to my right, tens of thousands of people scuttling about below us like ants, taxi drivers blasting their horns proprietorally. No mistaking where you were.

I was feeling particularly chipper, back in the city I had last visited on my J1 visa during the summer of my first year in college, and quickly relaxed into a stream of casual chat with Ellen.

1. *contd* hear from her again, but she seemed unperturbed by what she saw, and a few days later I got her digits, as they may or may not say Stateside. Which led to many a late-night phonecall on my part, in that New York is five hours behind Ireland time-wise and also because she had an actual job which necessitated she sit at a desk in the Chase Manhattan building downtown for twelve hours a day.

She was, however, a little anxious initially—she said so herself, extending her quivering hand, displaying her long, elegant piano-playing fingers. We laughed about the folly of our position, particularly mine, as I had travelled half-way round the world to go on a date with a woman I had never met before. (I had originally let it be known that I was due to visit New York around this time anyway, to catch up with my brother, who was there nearly every other weekend from the West Coast visiting his girlfriend, but as it turned out our schedules didn't merge as planned. With flights already booked, Ellen was in fact the only person I 'knew' in the city.)

Suitably refreshed after her vodka and cranberry juice, Ellen elected to take a shower before we went to dinner. I turned down an invitation to join her (I wish!), and elected instead to have a quick snoop at her bookshelf and CD collection to see what I could discern. A lot of non-fiction. A lot. Which I had expected, given some of the empirically-based rebuttals she had volleyed in my direction over the phone each night as I made successive and increasingly sweeping generalisations to support the position I held on whatever topic we were having a good natured argument about. Science and medical journals, books on economics, politics, global finance, evolution, psychology . . . the very antithesis of my own sagging shelves back home. This should be interesting, I thought to myself. Her extensive CD collection was a model of diversity, representative as it was of nearly every genre you could think of. And in some depth too, as evidenced by her chunky 40GB iPod, rendering my own 20GB one wafer thin in comparison. High-spec Technics stereo, ultra-high-end Panasonic HD TV, accompanied by *only* an equally impressive DVD player; no VCR: the girl had gone digital. Respect. And all the home entertainment gadgetry was to be enjoyed from the refined comfort of either a Le Corbusier LC2 sofa or LC4 recliner. Hard core design aesthetics at work here—this was looking good.

A careening cab ride down FDR took us to the East Village, where Ellen lived when she first came to New York. She had enjoyed the edgy, bohemian vibe there for two years or so, until the combined effects of sleep deprivation and her ascent up the corporate ladder necessitated a move to more tranquil pastures. We strolled around for a bit and then went to a small Italian place for a pizza. I must confess that I had, by this stage, assumed the role of interviewer and was, idiot that I am, probing ever deeper, looking for answers that might trigger some alarm within me, urging me to exercise due caution with the flame-haired, porcelain-skinned woman who had made quite an impression in a short space of time.

So. The SP: eldest of five children—one brother, three sisters, to whom she was very close and understandably protective of. Family unit only slightly dysfunctional, which these days amounts to functional. Good student, if a little wilful at times, but only mischievously so. Third-level education in Galway. Suitably disillusioned with the somewhat stifling parochial nature of modern Ireland and its people's continued over-reliance on alcohol as their sole social lubricant, she decamped to London to take up a job in finance. Pursued and attained a promotion entailing a move to New York. Strong work ethic ensured a steady and comparatively quick rise through the ranks, particularly admirable in light of her gender and the arena she worked in. Democrat. Gave up some of her time to teach literacy classes to disadvantaged kids. Card-carrying member of the Met. Devoted follower of arthouse films —was a regular patron of the very cool Angelika cinema in SoHo. Last book read—Michael Chabon's *The Amazing Adventures of Kavalier and Clay*.[2] Well informed about the world she lived in, excellent communicator, if a little semantic and infallible at times. Great sense of humour—loved *Curb Your Enthusiasm*. Social smoker. And cute. Really cute. What's not to like?.

Chuffed with the font of biographical and personal information I had gleaned so surreptitiously, I sat back and took a sip of wine.

'So, do I get the job?' Ellen asked matter-of-factly.

'Sorry?' I relied.

'The job. Have I got it?'

'What job?' I enquired, playing for time.

2. Strictly speaking, this didn't count as I had recommended it to her, but I gave her points for taking me up on the suggestion.

'Whatever one you just interviewed me for,' she said knowingly.

'We'll get back to you in a couple of days. There are a number of well-qualified candidates in the frame for the position, as I'm sure you can understand,' I said teasingly.

'Well, you have my contact details, so I'll wait to hear from you,' she said calmly, getting up as if to leave.

And then she left.

Walked right out of the restaurant, leaving me sitting there like a tit. I signalled the waiter, paid the bill quickly and hurried outside to find her leaning against the shutters of a deli a couple of doors down, smoking a cigarette.

'What's up?' I asked. Sincerely—not annoyed—this was a first.

'If I wanted to go for an interview, I'd have rung my agency, that's what's up. You were supposed to be having dinner with me, not compiling a background file for the CIA,' she replied sternly, the steely glint in her eyes letting me know that she was not a woman to be trifled with.

'Yeah, you're right. You're right. Sorry,' I said contritely. 'It's a habit I have. I have a thing about background information. I think it helps me underpin my instinctive feelings about someone. It's a total winner when I don't like someone—I get the bio and it reinforces the conclusion I've already jumped to. I suppose . . .'

'So what are you saying? You don't like me?' Ellen interrupted.

'No, no, no. Quite the opposite actually—I do like you. A lot. Which doesn't normally happen, and it's a bit freaky, so I suppose that's why I thought the bio might help cloud the blue sky a bit, you know?' I explained meekly.

'No, I don't know, to be honest with you. And yeah, it is a little freaky. It's a lot freaky. I'm just being me here, not playing any games, and I'd appreciate it if you could make a real big effort and do the same,' she said, stubbing her cigarette out on the pavement. Sorry, sidewalk.

'No problem,' I said, linking her arm affectionately. 'Let's get a drink.'

We ended up in The Scratcher, a comfy, well-worn dive located in a basement on East 5th Street and started lashing into Screwdrivers. (It would have been rude not to: they were only $4 a pop—well cheap by New York standards. Dublin's too.)

After an hour or so we were back on terra firma, enjoying a wide-ranging conversation just like the ones we had fallen into so easily on the phone in the preceding weeks.

A couple of hours later, we were both fairly drunk and standing outside sharing a cigarette. The vibe was right, so I figured it was as good a time as any to test the water. I went in for a bit of action and was met head on by the receptive Ellen. First base! And all it took was a 3,000-mile flight, her letting me know the way it was gonna be, and me not being a complete sap.

We split a cab uptown and after dropping her off at her building, I continued on through the park to my apartment on the Upper West Side, pleased with how things were developing so far. I called over to her place the next morning and we headed off to get some breakfast. The brother—a man who holds his breakfasting in similar high regard to myself—had tipped me off about EJ's, and thankfully there was one close by on Third Ave at 73rd Street. We settled into a booth and ordered—pancakes for Ellen and the special for me, shakes for both, with a caffeine jolt for the lady. Killer breakfast—totally set me up for the day.[3]

A good start is half the work as they say, and EJ's became the place where we started each day during my week in New York. After breakfast, we just hung out and did whatever felt right. We checked out lots of cool stuff—saw a great Brancusi exhibition at the Guggenheim, made a small dent in the permanent collection at the Met, checked out the Frick, had cocktails in The Campbell Apartment[4] in Grand Central. We lounged around in Bryant Square and Irving Plaza, lazily sipped a glass of wine in the private park in the elevated lobby of the uber-hip Hudson Hotel,[5] read

3. FYI, the special comprises two eggs cooked any style, served with home fries, choice of bacon, ham or sausage, and is accompanied by toasted challah (a yeast egg bread which is seriously delish), and preserves. Sure as hell beats a bowl of Ready Brek.

4. Formerly the private office and salon of 1920's tycoon, John W. Campbell, The Campbell Apartment was originally designed to reflect the galleried hall of a 13th-century Florentine palace. Recently restored to its original splendor, it is now a very cool cocktail lounge that is well worth a look.

books and argued constructively about loads of stuff whilst sitting on Ellen's favourite bench in Central Park. We hung out with her diverse group of very cool friends, went to see the Scissor Sisters in Irving Plaza, rode the 6 train downtown to do a bit of people-watching, crashed in her place and ordered in . . . You name it, we did it. All within reason of course.

The week wasn't without its setbacks though. Though with very similar—scarily similar—taste in a lot of things, it didn't take much for a harmless conversation to turn into quite a heated debate. The trouble with two people who think they know a lot about most things, and who most definitely have an opinion about everything, is that neither one likes to feel like the other has had the last word. I'd never met anyone like her for trenchantly defending her position on any given topic—from the insidious advances of globalisation to why Ireland sucks—and I liked her all the more for it, but the *way* we debated these topics was what gave me cause for concern.

I tire easily of constantly rationalising my apparently unorthodox views on many topics, and I can be a little curt and abrasive sometimes when I feel I'm covering old ground yet again. It's not cool really, but that's the way I am, and my pitifully small circle of friends are now resigned to my polemical tirades whilst atop any given hobby horse, but for someone new in my orbit, I suppose it can be quite uncomfortable and they might be liable to take personally what I say and the way I say it.

To compound matters, Ellen wasn't like this at all—she was a sensitive and highly sensitised individual who strove for inclusion and happy, well-informed consensus. She actually gave a shit about other people's opinions, whereas I am the kind of idiot who finds it difficult to understand why someone would have a partic-ular opinion when they were quite clearly wrong.

5. Totally recommended—across from Columbus and Central Park West, the Hudson is one of famed hotelier Ian Schrager's creations. It's a great place to chill midtown—45-foot trees (real ones), ivy-covered walls, and furnished with an eclectic collection of antique and modern garden furniture. You can smoke too. And, crucially, all the waitresses are absolutely gorgeous and wear just bikinis under-neath diaphanous sarongs.

The solution to this problem involved something I'm not particularly adept at either: compromise.

Ellen was a confident, evolved, sincere, intelligent, fun, formidable woman. She was indisputably attractive. I'd come across her like before. But this time was different: she liked me, warts and all. She told me so.

As I settled in for the long flight home I knew I was in unfamiliar territory.

18

W ww.newyork.craigslist.org/mnh/mis/ is one of my favourite URLS. Here you will find an amazing selection of 'missed connections' ads posted by New Yorkers desperate to get a second chance at making a first impression on someone they spotted as they went about the mundane business that is Life. For those of you not familiar with the sometimes weird but always wonderful world that is craigslist, let me bring you quickly up to speed.

In 1994, Craig Newmark was, as I regularly am, looking for ways to improve his social life. Unlike me though, Craig actually did something about it. He set up a regular e-mail bulletin, a list of cool events and happenings in the San Francisco Bay Area and started cc-ing it to his friends. His friends thought it was great, and they started cc-ing the list to their friends. The word spread and the list grew exponentially. Today, there are 120 'craigslists' in 25 countries around the world. Every month eight million users post five million free classified ads on the site, looking to let or sub-let an apartment, to sell some of their stuff, to promote an event, to post a CV, to offer 'exotic services' or to discuss the war in Iraq. The threads in the discussion forums alone—which cover topics as diverse as haiku, ecology, crafts, parenting, music, travel and TV—generate over one million postings every month. You name it, it's all happening on craigslist. And with so many users, there is, of course, a Personals section too, which makes for great reading when you're supposed to be working, especially the 'missed connections' category, which was added in 2000.

How about this:

> *We exchanged smiles while waiting for the light on Observer. You were in a small beige or silverish car. You were cute and I'd love to talk.*

Or this:

> *Hello. You sat beside me on the C train at around 1-1:15; I had a red backpack and had my headphones on. We looked at each other and we smiled a couple of times. I wish I had said something, but was feeling shy. You got off at the W4 stop. Drop me a line—would be interesting if this worked.*

Or this:

> *I can't believe I am doing this but it's driving me nuts . . . I have seen you in the morning a couple of times in Starbucks (the one on 71st & Continental), and passing me by on the street. I think you are so cute. I haven't seen you in a few days. I really would like to talk to you. I smiled at you quite a few times. Either you are not interested or have a girlfriend. If you are interested then I am letting you know that I am interested.*
>
> *You will probably never even see this . . . such a shame.*

Or this:

> *You got into a cab Friday on 14th Street and, I think, Second Avenue. We looked at each other. I still remember your pretty smile. Why did I have to be in a rush to get somewhere and not ask you to grab lunch with me? I have more time now and maybe I'll find you here.*

Being a writer of sorts, I find that, with some effective scheduling, I only have to leave the house once a week or so to take care of all the minutiae pertaining to my unfulfilling life. So with nothing better to do one Thursday, I thought I'd take off for the day and see if I couldn't get me a missed connection of my own.

First off, I got the LUAS into town from Dundrum. Nada. Probably didn't help that I was listening to my iPod, indicative as it is of contented isolation. Wandered around Stephen's Green and Dawson Street for a bit, but everybody seemed to be in such a hurry that there was no opportunity to catch a young lady's eye.[1] After an hour of that, I decided to go out to Blackrock, figuring there'd be some action at Pearse Station or on the DART itself. On the opposite platform I spotted a tall, slim woman, bedecked in a smart black suit and carrying a matching black leather portfolio. Thought she gave me a look all right, but she could have been just staring straight ahead, I suppose. She was heading northside anyway—it'd never work out. When I got to Blackrock it was humming with lunchtime activity. Even though I don't drink coffee, I got a cappuccino in Insomnia and pretended to read my book, glancing around casually every 14 seconds or so. No joy: too many alpha males in cheap suits sapping my *chi*.

A little disheartened, I headed for the station again, only to see a vision of loveliness sitting on a bench around the corner reading a book. Though the adjacent seat was empty I boldly sat down beside her, lit a cigarette and took out my book once again, stealing furtive glances in her direction as often as I could. Carefully tousled streaky short blonde hair. Tight white top underneath a cool jacket, with a scarf thrown casually around her neck. Three-quarter-length denim skirt with shiny black boots.

'Sorry, have you got a light please?'

She said.

To me.

What fool said smoking wasn't good for you?

'Sure thing,' I said, brandishing my trusty silver Zippo.

'Thanks,' she said, smiling warmly as she withdrew her cupped

1. Where are they all going? Freaks me out the way everybody's so busy.

hand from the flame. Totally brushed my hand too. Unintentionally maybe, but contact is contact.

'No problem. What are you reading?'

Please don't let it be the bloody *Da Vinci Code*.

'Oh cool, I read it a couple of weeks ago,' I said, examining the cover of Miriam Toews' *A Complicated Kindness*. 'Great book.'

'Yeah, I'm really into it. How 'bout you?'

She'd showed me hers, so I showed her mine—Jonathan Lethem's *Motherless Brooklyn*.

'Any good?'

'Yeah, it is. I've read some of his other stuff. He's great.'

An only slightly pregnant pause hung in the air. Exchanging names would be the next logical step, closely followed by the swapping of numbers and a firm commitment to meet for dinner later that evening after she had dumped whatever frat-boy jock she was currently—and mistakenly—involved with.

A car stopped. A horn honked. She looked up and waved to the female driver.

'Gotta go. 'Bye,' she said breezily. Tinged with regret too, I let myself think as she got into the car.

I returned home and logged onto craigslist to post my 'missed connection' ad. Now, us craigslisters are not stupid folk—we know that the chances of any of our rueful postings being read by those we wish to read them, are, obviously, incredibly slim. But we take comfort in at least being able to reassure ourselves that we did all we could to get in touch with the person concerned—we posted our digital message in bottle, and it's out there somewhere, bobbing up and down in cyberspace. But sometimes these missed connections manage, against seemingly insurmountable odds, to reconnect. The bottle washes up in the right place at the right time.

Take a brunette standing outside a Citibank branch on Flatbush Avenue. She's in her workout clothes, all sweaty after a spinning class or what have you. Whilst talking to a friend on her mobile, she spots this dude strolling down the street with a skateboard slung over his shoulder. She thinks he's fine and gives him a look, but doesn't feel up to saying hello on account of the fact that she's just out of the gym and doesn't feel terribly attractive in her smelly sweats. He checks her out too, before dropping his board and rolling off into the sunset, turning round once again to get another little look as he goes. Now, ordinarily that would be the end of it—it's something we can all identify with and probably have a similar tale of our own to contribute. But this particular tale didn't end there, no sir. The smelly brunette, one Rachel Mickenberg, a 32-year-old high school counselor, went home, had a shower and logged onto craigslist. She posted an ad under the heading 'to the cutie with skateboard on Flatbush Avenue', saying, 'I couldn't tell if you were looking at me because I was staring at you or because you were interested. If you are interested, get in contact'.

Lucky for Rachel, the intended recipient of her missive, one Jon Baker, also 32, is a craigslist enthusiast. Two days after she posted the ad, he was browsing the board, as you do, and two words jumped out at him—'skateboard' and 'Flatbush'. He sent a message to the anonymous poster, saying that he might be the guy she was looking for. Rachel replied and asked him to send a photo. He did. She opened the file and recognised the cutie from a few days previously. So the pair started mailing each other and a couple of weeks later decided to meet up. Whilst not necessarily blown away by each other on that first date, they hooked up again and after a few months decided that there was something there. Now, a good few months down the line, as they enjoy a lie-in on Saturday mornings reading the papers, they always make a point of checking out the postings on craigslist.

Great little story, isn't it? And I tell you one thing—there are few things I'd rather be doing on a Saturday morning than lying in bed, sifting through the review section of *The Guardian* whilst my sleepy-eyed, tousle-haired honey scanned through the latest postings on craigslist. It's a long shot, but hey, God loves a trier.

Needless to say, I was checking my mail even more regularly than usual in the days after my encounter. No message from my Blackrock honey as yet, but yesterday I decided to have a look at the Irish board of craigslist to see what was happening. Sod all, as usual,[2] but one ad in the women-seeking-men section did catch

2. The New York 'missed connections' board gets about 7,000 postings every month. The Dublin one? About 16. It's pathetic.

my eye. It was headed 'looking for an Irish man'. Pleased that I fitted the bill, I opened it up to have a read.

About you: smart, fun, witty, kind, and easy on the eyes. Someone who is confident, independent, and, like me, is looking for a partner to complement an already full life. Qualities I find particularly appealing include: a sense of adventure (be open-minded, own a passport, and know how to put it to use), an ability to enjoy life's simple pleasures, & a broad sense of humor. About me: I'm an incredibly boring clod with questionable values. My job as a professional jello wrestler is only a front to conceal my true occupation as the ringleader for an Italian shoe cartel. I love psychodrama, mind games, and am in need of constant stroking, coddling, and reassurance. I am lazy, slovenly, and really really stooopid. I am a great conversationalist as long as I am the only one talking. I run with scissors, swallow gum, eat pop rocks and drink soda at the same time, and I go swimming right after meals. Yes, I do know how to live on the edge . . .

You absolutely have to reply to an ad as cool as that, don't you? So I did. My opening message was jaunty and frivolous and included a photo of yours truly. And lo and behold, a couple of days later I get a mail headed, 'Hello Handsome' from a lady who included a photo of herself and quite cute she was too. Only snag was she lived in the US, in Nashville, Tennessee. She told me all about herself and seemed to be a perfectly well-balanced individual, happy enough with her lot in life, and looking to hook up with someone who shared her sunny disposition. Apart from the fact that I'm never really happy with my lot, not always of a sunny disposition and not particularly well balanced, I got where she was coming from, so I sent her another mail. Didn't receive a reply to it, and I wasn't expecting it to go anywhere really, but it was another iron in the fire as it were, so we'd see what happened.

Meanwhile, my star continued to rise ever higher in the Baltic regions. Relations between myself and Tatyana were developing apace, and I have to say, either she was very cleverly holding her cards close to her ample chest, or she genuinely wasn't that pushed about marrying a Westerner solely for naturalisation purposes, because she made no direct reference to visas and the like. The content of our e-mails had been fairly wide-ranging, with each of us swapping details about our jobs, families, backgrounds, interests and related matters. Tatyana appeared to be a very independent woman, being the only member of her large family to have left her hometown in search of opportunities elsewhere. She was refreshingly frank when discussing men, what she wanted and expected of them and what she felt she has to offer in return, and seemed to have given up all hope of finding a suitable partner in Belarus. She told me she was 'looking for someone to know first; then try to make a serious relationship'. Her dream was to have 'one who will love, care and have respect for me as his wife', because, 'the men we have here do not respect their wives', in light of the fact that apparently, 'there are more than enough beautiful but lonely women, so the men keep looking outside', the dirty dogs.

Needless to say, Paul was making a strong case on Tatyana's behalf, fearful as he was of seeing the season end without any 'silverware'. When I called over to his place for a pep talk, he laid out his suggestions for our future gameplan.

'Forget this kerbcrawling lark, Do. You can't be cruising around the city on the off-chance some chick gives you a look. I wouldn't mind if you had a crack at them there and then, but posting it on the Net in the hope that they see it and get in touch with you? That's far too random. Seriously, man, it's time we stopped messing around. We're all over the place, there's no shape to what we're doing here.'

'So what are you suggesting?'

'I'll tell you what I'm suggesting: Forget about Ireland and the UK. Look to the East, my friend. It's freezing—they're all dying to get out of there; the vast majority of them are out-and-out stunners; the blokes they have to put up with over there are complete morons by the sounds of it, which means they'll be fairly low maintenance . . . There's a lot to be said for it.'

'I know what you mean, but it's a tricky one to get your head around all the same.'

'I really think we should we try something with Tatyana,' he urged.

'There's plenty I'd like to try with Tatyana, don't you worry,' I replied wistfully. Did you check out the photo of her at the beach I sent you?'

'Too right; she's a cracker, no doubt about it. Rach wasn't too impressed though.'

'That's a bit petty really, isn't it? No offence, now, I know she's your wife and all that, but she's probably jealous.'

'I don't mean like that, you tit. No, what happened was she arrived home from her sister's and there's me, checking out the photo on the laptop while I was giving the little fella a feed. She didn't think it was 'appropriate''

'You're shitting me? It's not like she was naked. And he's only a couple of months old.'

'My point exactly. Be nice if she was though,' Paul said longingly, reaching for his ringing phone.

'Was that Rachel?' I inquired when he rang off.

'Yeah. She was in Louise's for some girly dinner thing. On her way home now.'

'I'm off so,' I said, anxious not to be there when she returned in case Paul landed me in yet another awkward conversation with her, something he seemed to have quite a prodigious talent for.

'Not a word to Rachel about any of this, right? Nothing will probably come of it anyway.'

'Mum's the word. You're something of a *persona non grata* with her at the minute anyway.'

'What have I done now, for God's sake?'

'It's Ben, you know? She's still narked with herself for having left him with you—she didn't think you were up to it. And now she's convinced he's different with her since the weekend.'

'Lovely. He's still alive, isn't he?' I said exasperatedly. 'I fed him and walked him and played with him, did everything she told me to. And you better not buckle and tell her about the name-change thing.'

'I won't,' Paul snorted disgustedly. 'Be more than your life's worth. And mine. She actually said she thought the dog had 'abandonment issues', can you believe that?'

'With Rachel, I can believe anything. Good luck. Bye García.'
'Careful.'

Maybe Paul had a point, I thought, as I sped along the motorway on my way home. Not about Tatyana being naked—everything in good time—but about rationally examining the possibility of meeting her. It's not like she was an alien or anything: if we clicked, we clicked; if we didn't, we didn't.

19

I decided to place an ad of my own in the 'Connections' section of *The Irish Times*. After dialling 1570 562999 I listened to a few of the messages other people had left, so as to get an idea how folks were selling themselves. At €1.75 a minute I didn't dally too long, though. I then called 1800 925046, and after securing a username and password, I quickly recorded my own jaunty little message on the system, and promptly forgot about the whole thing, consumed as I was with my online activities. Then one day, after I had returned home from a long weekend in the country, I got a text message from a woman called Alison. It took me a while to figure out who she was or where she might have gotten my number from, but the penny dropped eventually.[1]

Keen to explore this new option, I texted Alison back there and then, and about half an hour later another message arrived from her. I composed another reply, though even at that early stage I was beginning to tire of the format: texting just doesn't do it for

---

1. Curiously, her message said she 'saw' my ad. I say curiously because it meant that my voice ad had obviously been transcribed by some lackey for publication in the newspaper. I eventually managed to get a hold of a copy of the previous Friday's paper to see how the printed version had fared in its transition. Sure enough, it had lost something of its originality and spontaneity, but what the heck, I figured, it gave me greater exposure.

me really—the logistics of it don't permit you to express yourself as you might like to, given the necessity for brevity and shorthand. Additionally, my right hand was quickly developing symptoms of RSI due to my never having mastered the predictive-text facility on my mobile, despite the extensive tutorials I had received from my 13-year-old nephew. Alison kept at it, though, and after the fourth long message I decided to throw caution to the wind and just ring her, confident that I'd know within two minutes if I ever wanted to send her another text message, let alone actually meet her.

Approximately one minute and forty seconds later, I knew I couldn't be arsed with her. Sounding genuinely a little miffed, Alison said I had put her 'on the spot' by ringing her and that she didn't 'know what to say'. Hardly a good sign of how things might pan out were we to meet in person for a drink, I thought. If you can't open up and have a chat when afforded the protective insulation of a telephone line, how scintillating can you hope to be when you're face to face with someone? I eventually got a bit of info out of her: she told me she worked in the civil service; and that she lived in a house she had bought with her sister, who was a teacher.

'Oh, right,' I said, trying to sound interested. 'And whereabouts is the house?'

'D'ya know Wilton?' she said to me.

'You mean Wilton in *Cork*?' I asked incredulously.

'Sure there's only da wan Wilton,' she said, equally incredulously.

One more than we need. Cork—if she'd told me was she was a body double for Natalie Portman I wouldn't have gone near her. Time to wrap this one up. I walked over to the microwave and set the timer for ten seconds, holding my mobile beside it when the bell finally came to my rescue.

'Is dat yor dinner?' Alison asked.

Bright as button and no mistake.

'It sure is. I'm only in the door and I'm starving. I just thought I'd give you a quick ring to say hello, you know? So I'll go now, and maybe we'll talk again, yeah?' I said encouragingly.

'Oh. Oh, okay so. Bye.'

'Bye.'

Click. Dial tone.

Of all bloody places, I thought to myself as I looked forlornly at my empty microwave, wishing there really was a braised lamb steak from Suppers Ready in there. I'd a good mind to get on to *The Irish Times* classifieds and suggest they introduce some sort of filtering system, allowing you the option of blocking numbers from certain areas, so you wouldn't have to go through that kind of ordeal. Though I had no inclination whatsoever to get to know Alison any further, I took the precaution of storing her number in my phone so I wouldn't be caught off guard in case she thought our little chat had gone well and decided to give me a ring, appending the phone number with a suitably cautionary tag in lieu of her actual name.[2] An hour later I got another text, but it was only Paul, checking in to see how things were going.[3]

The following day I got another text message; from a different number, mercifully. This particular woman was all business, and asked me to forward her 'all details' about myself, if you don't mind. I replied with some of the requested information, finishing up by asking her where she was from herself: the Philippines. That was much better, I thought to myself. A couple of texts later established that the young woman, Anna, was 34 years old and was employed as a childminder for a family in south County Dublin. She came across as very pleasant, and seemed keen to meet up as soon as possible, letting me know that Sunday and Monday were her days off. Pleased at not having to maintain a texting-based relationship for too long, I readily agreed and let her know that Sunday was fine by me. She suggested we meet outside The Gresham Hotel at three o'clock. O'Connell St is far from my favourite place in Dublin city centre, but I guessed she might not know her way around too well and said that was fine.

On Sunday I stood opposite the Gresham until I spotted Anna from across the road and strolled over to introduce myself. She was very shy and quietly spoken, and though it was a cool enough November afternoon she wore a pair of tinted vanity glasses. I suggested we head southwards and find somewhere quiet to have a drink and a chat. She smiled agreeably and we set off down the

2. **CORK**

3. any crack wit de fone sex lark?

street. We exchanged polite small-talk as we walked, though I couldn't help notice quite a few people casting dubious looks in my direction as I walked alongside the petite, dark-skinned Filipina, their eyes tacitly accusing me of having paid an introductions agency in Manila to secure to her safe arrival on my doorstep.

I took her to the upstairs bar in The Central Hotel on Exchequer Street where we found a table in the corner just as a few people were leaving. I got a glass of wine and Anna, not being a drinker at all, had a cup of tea. The conversation was slow enough in developing, with me doing all the running in order to avoid long silences between my polite questions and Anna's concise answers. Whilst not deliberately in my customary biographical mode, I figured a few general questions about her situation here would help break the ice. Turned out she had been in Ireland for over two years, and was presently employed by a decent family in Glenageary. There were four children in the family, ranging in age from 2 to 8, though the two youngest ones were her primary focus. Anna had her own little studio apartment in the garden of what sounded like a large detached house, and her duties and responsibilities were clearly defined. She had two days off every week and also accompanied the family on holidays, both in Ireland and abroad. Amidst all you hear of non-national workers being exploited by unscrupulous agencies and companies, I was pleased to hear that her regime did not sound unduly onerous. She was quick to point out that this was not the same for other Filipinas she knew in Dublin, and that her own situation had only improved in the past few months after she had negotiated with the parents exactly what she was prepared to do and for how much.

Gradually feeling a little more relaxed in my company, Anna was nothing less than direct when it came to her turn to ask me a few questions.

How many replies did you get to your ad?
Are you going to meet many of the women?
When?
Do you like Irish women or prefer women from other countries?
Are you married?

Have you ever been married?

Do you live with anybody?

Do you have your own money?

Do you have to support anybody else?

Do you like children?

I answered the questions honestly and candidly, somewhat amused by her frankness, though unsure of where it stemmed from or the motivation behind it. She certainly wasn't looking for a visa—she was working here in a perfectly legal capacity.

She appeared to be a confident and independent woman who was used to working to support herself, so I didn't get the feeling she was looking for a ticket to the easy life either. Thankfully, my curiosity was satisfied a few minutes after my Q&A session, when Anna announced that she had to go.

'Oh, okay,' I said a little surprised, wondering which of the many no-doubt-unsuitable answers I had given her had most wounded my prospects.

'I must meet somebody else at six o'clock,' she said firmly.

'I see. A friend of yours, is it?' I probed casually.

'No. It is another man whose ad I replied to,' she told me.

'Right. God, you're having a busy day, aren't you?' I said, smiling playfully.

'No, not at all,' Anna answered demurely, bowing her head, a little embarrassed by my imputed suggestion.

'I'm only messing, don't worry,' I said, rowing back quickly, lest she thought I was actually suggesting her conduct was improper. 'It was very nice to meet you, Anna,' I continued, extending my hand. 'If you want to meet again, you have my number, so I'll leave it to you to get in touch if you'd like, okay?'

'Okay. It was nice to meet you too. Goodbye.'

And off she went to meet her next suitor. I must admit I was a little thrown by the business-like nature of her questions, but I put it down to her maybe having met up with a number of men in the past who strung her along for a while, feeding her all sorts of bullshit about their honourable intentions, declarations which a comparatively innocent and decidedly virtuous woman such as herself might be inclined to believe.

For a variety of reasons, I didn't envisage anything happening between myself and Anna after our first meeting, so I was a little surprised when she sent me another text message the following Tuesday, enquiring as to whether or not I would like to meet her again that coming Sunday. I said I would, partly out of curiosity, but mostly because I didn't want to her to think that I felt she was unsuitable for me in some way. It's difficult to explain really. I suppose I didn't want her to think her I was racist in any way, however melodramatic that may sound. She had told me a little of her background and it was clear that it had been an uphill battle all the way for her to get to where she now was, and the last thing I wanted was for her to feel that some privileged Paddy regarded her as being less than worthy relationship material.

Sunday rolled around; I met Anna as scheduled and took her for lunch to The Gotham Café. (I felt like a break from The Market Bar.) Over pizza she told me more about her formative years, and the more she told me, the more I knew that I was the last person she should be considering getting involved with.[4] After a long, lazy lunch, which I gladly paid for, we went for a short walk

4. When she was 7-years-old Anna was dispatched from her home in San Mateo to be brought up by a family in Manila, some 350kms away. Allowed to attend school three days a week in return for doing domestic chores, she did not see any of her family again until she was 21, by which time her father had died. When her mother finally tracked her down in the capital, she brought her back to San Mateo. Anna's many siblings had grown up, barely realising they had a sister. She couldn't settle in her home town and eventually made her way to Hong Kong, where she completed a course in childcare, working as a cleaner to support herself. She came to Ireland as a professional nanny in early 2002. From the day she received her first paycheck, Anna began sending money to her family in the Philippines via a remittance centre in the city centre. Through her generosity, her extended family had been able to move from apparently near-slum-like conditions to a properly constructed private house with all modern facilities. Anna had returned home to spend Christmas with her family in 2002, and had not been back since then. Her mother died at the age of 56 shortly after Anna came back to Ireland. She wasn't able to go home for the funeral, and had not been back since.

around the Grafton Street area. She loved to window shop with her friends there, only actually buying clothes when necessary, and always in the sales. I was both struck and not a little humbled by her virtue and values, and told her so. She allowed herself an embarrassed smile but said nothing.

When I playfully enquired how her second meeting had gone the previous Sunday, she laughed and said that the man in question was 'quite nice, but too old'. I did a bit of gentle probing about her relationship expectations and quickly surmised that Anna was simply exploring the romantic options open to her in her adopted homeland. After a lifetime of working hard to support others, and constantly putting the needs of her family before her own, she was finally allowing herself the opportunity to see what possibilities Ireland, and Irish men, could hold. I knew I was far from what she needed, and set about telling her so, in as polite and considerate a manner as I could. She graciously accepted without question everything I said and we parted company a short while later when I walked her to her bus stop. After bidding her farewell and wishing her luck, I urged her to feel free to get in touch with me again if she felt there was anything I could help with. I meant it sincerely, and she said she would, but I think she was just being her customary polite self.

Not having bothered to renew my ad in the paper for the following week, my mobile was mercifully quiet and I returned to cyberspace, turning my attention once again to Tatyana in Belarus. She was all on for meeting up face to face to take things to the 'next level', though I was sure that my interpretation of what constituted the next level differed slightly from hers. (And from Paul's.[5]) In her most recent e-mail, Tatyana had said, *'I will want to know you closer for no one knows what the future may have for both of us.'* Only one way to find out, so I bit the bullet and said I was happy to meet up with her at some point in the not-too-distant

5. Idiot that he is—*married* idiot that he is—Paul had actually gone and joined DatingDirect himself the previous week. Understandably enough, Rachel had a fit when she found him cruising profiles one Saturday morning, jogging his first-born on his knee as he sought out potential mates on my behalf.

future. She replied the next day, delighted with the suggestion and we settled on Frankfurt as a meeting point. I booked a flight and a hotel really quick before I thought about it too much and changed my mind. (Paul was ecstatic, much to my amusement and Rachel's consternation. So much so that at one point I was waiting for him to suggest he come along with me.)

Coming up on the inside though, in the now-hotly contested race to win my heart, was newcomer Anya. Anya was 28, lived in St Petersburg,[6] had shoulder-length blonde hair, green eyes, modestly described herself as 'attractive', when in fact she was a total honey, and most impressively, stood a statuesque 6 feet tall.[7] She worked in the tourism industry, spoke English and Italian as well as her native Russian, and liked 'travelling, as well as having fun, reading books, going to cinema, cooking and sleeping till noon on weekends'. Not backwards about coming forward, Anya made it clear in her profile that she was looking for a husband: *'I like to meet HIM!'*

Gregarious chap that I am, I sent a message to Anya, acknowledging receipt of hers and telling her a little about myself. Quick off the ball, she was back in touch the following day with a cheery

6. St Petersburg, formerly known as Leningrad and Petrograd, lies on delta of the river Neva at the eastern end of the Gulf of Finland on the Baltic Sea. Founded by Tsar Peter the Great in 1703, it served as the capital of the country during its imperial period until 1918, and today is home to some 4.7 million people, making it the second largest city in the Russian Federation. Given its key role in history, the city is adorned with many magnificent buildings, and is often referred to as the City of Palaces, the most notable of all, perhaps, being the splendidly baroque Winter Palace, home of the Hermitage Museum. According to the results of the last census, released on 9 October 2002, the average monthly salary in the city is €176. (And I thought I was broke.) Curiously, people can only move to St Petersburg once they can prove they have a job and a room, or if they are married to an inhabitant of St Petersburg. The city is a major centre for machine building, manufacturing, printing, shipping, and increasingly, tourism. Have to say, after checking out a few sites to bring myself up to speed with the place, I quite fancied a trip there—it looked absolutely beautiful.

7. You can climb any tree when it's down, as the man says.

follow-up message, enquiring as to what my 'planning' was. A spade was most definitely a spade in the Baltics.

A couple of days later, I was over in Paul's house once again. Rachel was there this time, but opened the door with a warm smile, which was a good sign—looked like we were back on solid ground after a somewhat testing time. She had not been my most vocal supporter over the past couple of months. It wasn't that she didn't like me, though; it was just that she seemed to feel sorry for the women I had dated.

'For your eyes only,' Paul said gravely, handing me a document wallet while Rachel was making coffee.

'What's this?'

'This, my friend, is The Frankfurt File. In there you'll find everything you need for your trip. Hotels, bars, cool clubs, good restaurants, maps . . . you name it, it's all there. Slipped in a bit on the red light district too—you never know, she might be a bit gamey that way. And if she is, we want to capitalise on it. I did it at work today. Took me a couple of hours as well, so make good use of it, yeah?'

'I'll have a look at it later,' I said, trying to sound grateful. He really was getting a bit carried away with all this.

'Lovely. Thanks hon,' he said as Rachel joined us with freshly brewed coffee. 'Any Toffee Crisps?'

'Yeah, they're in the press beside the fridge,' she said, flopping down on the sofa. 'You know, in the kitchen? The room with the sink and the cooker? It's just through there.'

'Right, right,' Paul said, resting his cup on the window sill before extricating himself from his La-Z-Boy. 'One for everyone in the audience, yeah?'

'So when are you off to meet Tatyana?' Rachel asked me.

'Three weeks or so. Though the more I think about it, the less I want to go,' I confided.

'Why's that?'

'I think she's of the opinion that if we meet up face to face for a few days and have a laugh that, all going well, I'm basically going to suggest she move to Ireland, you know? It's a bit mad really.'

'That's certainly the outcome Paul is banking on. He's invested a lot of time and energy in you, you know?' she said mockingly, obviously repeating a line he had trotted out to her.

'What's this?' he said, returning with the chocolate treats.

'I was just asking Donal how he was fixed for the trip to Germany,' Rachel replied innocently.

'No worries there. We're all set. Back of the net this time, isn't that right?' he said emphatically.

'Yeah. Maybe,' I answered quietly, my lack of conviction going unnoticed as Paul tried to wrestle the remote control from Rachel's grip.

'And I believe Ellen's home this weekend?' Rachel said, conceding defeat. 'How are things going there?'

'Ellen's cool and the gang,' Paul said quickly on my behalf, 'but we're not sure if it's a winner in the long run, you know? She's hard work. Bit of an overachiever, if you ask me.'

'Which I didn't,' Rachel said sternly. 'Donal, what's the story with Ellen?'

'Hard to tell really, Rachel. She is cool, I like her a lot, and I know she likes me, despite how odd that may sound to you, but it's not very practical, is it? Her in New York and me here. And it's not so much that *she's* hard work—which she is, but mostly in a good way—it's more that the whole relationship thing is hard work, you know?'

'I know they are,' Rachel said, nodding her head in Paul's direction. 'But if you can see something there that's worth holding onto, then it doesn't feel like work. It feels right. And then making that jump to the next level isn't so scary,' she said, her six years of experience with Paul no doubt informing her opinion.

Bloody jumps and levels—that was all I was hearing these days.

20

'You're entrenched,' Ellen said affirmatively as we walked down the street.

'I'm where?' I enquired bemusedly.

'Entrenched. You're entrenched. You can't share.'

'Excuse me? Who paid for dinner in Il Primo last night?'

'Not like that, you idiot. You can't share *you*. You're too set in your ways. Any interruption to your precious routines and you seize up . . .'

'That's rubbish. I've no idea what you're talking about,' I retorted defensively.

'What was all that this morning then, about your 'breakfasting routine'? It's pathetic . . .' she mocked.

'It's more of a brunching thing actually,' I said sniffily, 'and like I said . . .'

'Whatever. I think it's entrenched. And I just don't know if I can be with somebody like that . . .'

The end was in sight. I could feel it coming. There might not be any need for us to have 'the talk' that a couple of weeks ago seemed to be looming large on the horizon. (Perversely, for one who normally runs a mile from commitment, I was rather looking forward to it: I've never had one of these conversations before, you see. The outcome of these long and involved, cards-on-the-table, heart-on-your-sleeve discussions can have serious repercussions for years to come, and part of me felt I was missing out on participating in what seemed to be a very grown up thing.) But if it wasn't meant to be, then it wasn't going to be.

Anyway, that was a low blow indeed—taking a potshot at one of my routines. Most people have their predetermined routines every day, which they go through by rote, hardly noticing the beneficial effect they have in putting some class of structure on their day. However, single and without gainful employment as I am, I have no pre-ordained conventions which I must adhere to daily to satisfy a third party, be it a wife, child or line manager. To combat the possible long-term detrimental effects of this situation—i.e. achieving even less than usual every day—I resolved some time ago to adopt a couple of routines of my own invention and stick to them steadfastly, in an effort to put some sort of 'structure' on my 'working' day. My brunching routine is the very bedrock on which said structure is built. If it goes awry, the day can be written off in its entirety, over before it's even begun.

Abhorrent of culinary effort and excess as I am, I have over the years developed a schedule of operations which delivers me a hearty noon-time platter with the minimum of fuss.[1] It's a model of substance and efficiency, the only failing of which, if indeed it could be called that, is this: it is simply not scalable. Were another

1. Birds Eye waffles and fish fingers—two of each—on a baking tray and into a preheated oven for 14 minutes. Three minutes thereafter two Shaws 80% pork sausages into a pan with a little olive oil—extra virgin—followed four minutes later by two thick-cut Denny Maple Cure back rashers, when the alarm on my mobile phone reminds me to turn waffles/fish fingers. Kerrygold butter retrieved from fridge and set beside toaster to soften a little. Large glass of low-fat milk poured and set on table. 200g tin of Heinz baked beans into a saucepan. Two slices of Brennan's wholegrain bread lowered into toaster and set to brown just shy of level four. Two minutes later the alarm sounds once more and in a few deft movements and a matter of seconds my plate is laden with fare fit for a builder from Mayo. The Noah's Ark as I like to call it: two of everything. (Apart from the beans that is, of which there are approximately 73.)

present in the house, it would mean either performing the operation twice—thereby bringing untold levels of stress upon myself, to the extent that I would not even be able to enjoy my own bit of grub—or dividing in two the product of a single production run, which would leave me unsatisfied, ill-prepared for the day ahead and more-than-a-little annoyed with the intruder who forced such a compromise. In effect, no accommodations can be made for guests, regardless of the level of intimacy which may have been achieved in the small hours preceding it.

And this is what Ellen was referring to when she said I was 'entrenched', a position made all the more untenable as we were having this very conversation on the way back from Café Assisi on Thomas Street—purveyors of *the* finest breakfast paninis. And *I* paid for them. What was she like?

This episode was unfortunately the latest in a string of unfortunate events that had unfolded between us over the few days we spent together when she was home in November. I had been looking forward to seeing her again; mostly because I liked her a lot, but partly because I wanted to see if there was any real substance to our relationship, if it could survive a honeymoon period and blossom into something lasting.[2] After a somewhat stuttering start, we were getting on pretty well, though I was beginning to realise that Ellen had quite a few buttons which, when pressed even ever so slightly, brought forth a side to her that I didn't much care for. I had picked up on this during some of our long phonecalls, but chalked it down to the fact that she was in New York working hard in a very stressful environment, I was in Dublin, hardly working at all, and that phonecalls are not the best medium through which to develop a relationship, lacking in visual contact, body language and intimacy as they are.

2. I hate Christmas, and was pleased to discover that Ellen regarded it with similar disdainful antipathy. To this end, I had decided to spend Christmas of 2004 in sunny Spain, away from all the madness, excess and enforced jollity in Dublin. I had mentioned my plans to Ellen on the phone a couple of weeks before her return to Dublin, and she said she'd join me down there. But now, things between us were looking shaky. Typically, I had gotten ahead of myself a little and already booked my ticket and reserved a car.

As our time together had progressed, though, I got the feeling that the relationship couldn't last in its present form. Apart from the geography thing, which was a major issue for Ellen, I sensed that she had a problem with being wrong. And I'm not talking about wrong in the sense of having a stupid opinion on something, which I can handle if it's expressed in an articulate manner and founded on some body of empirically sound knowledge. Maybe wrong is even the wrong way to describe it, actually. It's more like she had a problem with accepting that the utterance of another could in fact be right, and she was a bit narked that she didn't already know whatever it was that was under discussion, as if accepting that someone else could be in possession of some knowledge, however innocuous and non-threatening to her place in the world, implied a weakness or deficiency on her part. It's difficult to explain really. You'd have to be there, and since you weren't, you're just going to have to take my word for it. A representative example should help throw some light on the matter.

We were in town one of the days, strolling happily around for a couple of hours, not doing anything of particular note, when my belly announced that it was in need of sustenance. I suggested that we go to the Market Bar (where else?), for a bite to eat. Ellen agreed and we made our way to Fade Street. She had never been there before and was suitably impressed with the large bright, airy space it was. We took a seat at one of the long tables and she perused the menu. After deciding on what she was going to have, she took a long look around her surroundings, nodding her approval at the stripped back décor.

'I really like all those clogs they have up on that display,' she said.

'Yeah, it's cool. They're not clogs though. They're lasts,' I said, correcting her.

'Sorry?'

'They're not clogs. They're lasts. Shoemakers use them to build up the shoe. If a shoe is the positive, a last is the negative, you know?'

'I know what a last is,' she said a little acidly.

'Fair enough, I'm just telling you that they're lasts. Not clogs.'

'Are you sure?' she asked me, not seeming too comfortable with the prospect of me knowing something she didn't.

'Trust me. I'm in here, like, once a week, they're definitely lasts,' I said assuredly.

'Hmmm,' Ellen hmmmed, not actually conceding the point. 'I wonder how many of them there are.'

'421,' I said.

'What?'

'421. I counted them.'

'When? Just now?' she asked in disbelief.

'No, not just now. Ages ago. Like I said, I'm in here quite a bit.'

A breezy American arrived to take our order, puncturing the slightly tense atmosphere that had developed. After we ordered, Ellen excused herself to go to the bathroom, the door to which was at the far end of the bar, right underneath the now-contentious display of lasts affixed to the brick wall. As she walked slowly towards the bathroom I just knew she was trying to count the bloody things, hoping I was wrong so she could correct me on her return. I was fully aware of how hard she had to work to get where she was in life, particularly being a woman in a traditionally male-dominated arena, but you had to be able to leave certain stuff in a certain place and just relax. What did it matter how many lasts there were on the wall? I happened to know how many there were because I eat there more than I should and I counted the bloody things one day whilst waiting for my spicy meatballs.

'So. Did you count them?' I asked her on her return.

'Count what?'

'Doesn't matter.'

I see. You didn't have enough time to count them without my noticing, so you're letting on you weren't counting them at all. Very mature, I thought to myself, tiring of her incessant competitive streak. An awkward few moments passed before the arrival of our food, giving us something else to talk about.

That kind of thing.

There was definitely a lot about Ellen that I liked and that I knew I wouldn't find too quickly in most other women, but unfortunately these attractive qualities carried a hefty surcharge. One that I knew I wouldn't be able to pay in the long term. And so it was with something approaching a heavy heart—for I know not the exact weight of a truly heavy heart—that I said goodbye to her at the airport early on that Wednesday morning. Her work schedule did not permit another visit home for quite some time and the credit limit on my Visa card did not permit me another trans-Atlantic jaunt for quite some time.

'Bye, Ellen. Take care,' I said, kissing her affectionately.

'I will. You too. Bye Donal.'

We hugged tightly and then she turned to go. As I watched her go through the departure gates, I knew I probably wouldn't ever see her again.

———

Five days later . . .

———

Well, that was it. Ellen and I were no longer an item. I certainly saw it coming when she was home, and I'm sure she had her doubts as well. For whatever reason, I don't think either of us wanted it to end when she was here, but it ended a couple of nights later on the phone. Not acrimoniously I'm glad to say, but after a long and sincere talk which went on well into the night. Ellen was great, is great, in so many ways, but for something to work out between us in the long run required quite a leap on both our parts, literally as well as figuratively. In fairness to her, she seemed willing to jump, but something in the back of my mind told me that we wouldn't make it. And I didn't want to fall.

———

'Not to worry, mate,' Paul said reassuringly when we met in Mulligan's the day after the night before. 'We've still got our ace in the hole. In a few days' time, we could be top of the table again.'

'I don't think so. I've decided not to go. I sent Tatyana a mail this evening to let her know.'

'What? What did you that for, you moron? We were all set.'

'It just felt a bit weird. She's looking for a husband and a better life; here, the UK, the States, wherever. It's too clinical, the whole thing. You're a boy, I'm a girl, let's meet in Frankfurt and see how we get on? Nah, I'm not into it anymore. I'm getting sick of this whole thing, to be honest with you, barking up every tree looking for a date. I'm happy enough with me the way I am. If I meet someone and they hang around long enough to realise that I'm not a complete tit, then well and good. If they don't, then it's their loss,' I said determinedly.

'Fair enough, Do, but we've come so far now, do you not think you should just go and check it out? Maybe she's really cool, and you'll get on really well. Have you thought about that?' Paul reasoned, urging me to reconsider my decision.

'I have, yeah. And you're right, maybe she is really cool. But even still, there's something manufactured and contrived about the whole thing. I'm just tired, you know? I've been at this shit for nearly a year. It's time to move on.'

'Right, so. You're not into it any more, I can see that. Looks like I'll have to tender my resignation.'

'Looks that way. I'd be glad to offer you a pint of Guinness in recognition of all your efforts. More than they're worth, obviously, but it's the kind of guy I am, you know?'

21

I had initially thought about staying in Dublin for the Christmas break but finally decided against it, figuring that after breaking up with Ellen and deciding against going to Frankfurt to meet Tatyana, the time away would do me good. It had been quite a manic year, what with all the to-ing and fro-ing, riding the rollercoaster of 'love', so on 21 December I hopped on a plane to Malaga and headed for my sister's apartment once again. And I have to say, in all honesty, I had a grand old time. It was a pleasant change to get through the seasonal holidays in a pair of shorts underneath a blue sky. I brought a stack of books with me, along with a list of movies to watch that I'd missed in the cinema.

I had of course, plenty of time to reflect on the ups and downs of the previous ten months or so while I was there. Whilst not regretful of the lengths I had gone to on my quest for a soulmate/lover/girlfriend/partner/confidante, on the whole, I concluded that the more I went looking for whatever I thought it was that I was looking for, the less likely it was that I was going to find it. If it was going to happen, it was going to happen.

———

204

And then it happened.

———

I was no sooner home than I wanted to get away again, with the result that I spent the first two weeks of January 2005 looking for ways to get out of Ireland for the second two weeks of January 2005. I had been toying with the idea of going to Barcelona for a year to teach English and was doing some research on the Net when I came across a site called vaughanvillage.com. A company called Vaughan Systems ran intensive English learning courses in Spain, sequestering twenty or so Spaniards and a similar number of native English speakers away in a small village a couple of hours west of Madrid for a week at a time. On offer to any English speaker willing to speak for fourteen hours a day: free transfer from a pick-up point in Madrid plus bed and board (including wine), for the week and return transfer to Madrid the following Friday. What's not to like? I filled in the fairly cursory application form online and zapped it off to HQ. The very next day I received an e-mail back from them, telling me they'd be delighted if I could participate and asking me to select a week and a location (they have three different centres), that would suit me best.

I opted for a tiny village called Valdelavilla tucked away in the province of Soria, near the famous Rioja wine region, about three hours north-east of Madrid. Rarely having to check a calendar before committing to something, I then quickly selected the next three consecutive weeks and let them know of my choices. They confirmed receipt of my details and that was that.

But then I changed my mind about the location. Whilst checking out the site for further information I came across the second location they used—a place called Barco de Avila, near the border of Salamanca and Cáceres, about two-and-a-half hours west of Madrid—and noticed that this programme took place in a hotel located on its own grounds in a restored country house and stables. Four stars it was too—room service, leisure centre, the lot. Not having cause to stay in such refinement too often, especially when someone else is paying for it, I asked to switch location. They said that was cool, but only if I could go for the second week I had chosen, not the first. Fine by me. I clicked onto aerlingus. com, booked a flight for €100, promptly forgot about the whole thing and got on with doing very little, as is my wont. The day of my departure arrived and I headed off into the unknown.

The company had organised a tapas reception for the twenty or so participating Anglos in a bar in central Madrid the night before the programme kicked off, and when I arrived, I was overcome with a desire to make for the airport and head back home: way too many loud Americans for my liking, nobody else my age, and all assembled were generally of that manic happy disposition I associate with cult members awaiting the arrival of their leader in a spaceship atop a mountain in the desert 'round midnight.

I lurked around the perimeter of the festivities, had a couple of glasses of wine, and surveyed my fellow teachers, assessing whether or not I could handle being isolated in a remote country hotel for a week, with them as my only company. As I was inwardly cursing the lengths I was willing to go to for four stars and three squares a day, one of the coordinators spotted me and dragged me over to meet a few people. Naturally enough, most of them turned out to be perfectly pleasant—just not necessarily my kind of people. I quizzed Maria on what level of interaction I was expected to have with my fellow tutors. Not much, she said comfortingly—the idea was to spend as much time as possible talking to the Spaniards. A little reassured I made my excuses and split to my hostel for a terrible night's sleep.

I arrived in good time at the pick-up point the following day and took a seat on a nearby bench, from which vantage point I could scrutinise and pre-judge both the Anglos and Spaniards as they arrived to meet the coach.

And then I saw her.

She was about 5'5" tall. Slim. Long, lustrous dark brown hair falling over a quilted three quarter length white coat worn over a polo neck sweater. Black trousers and heels. Looked about 28 or so. That was all I could see, but it was enough. She had a look about her that I knew I liked.

The coach was about to move off. Having now decided not to abscond in a taxi, I strolled over and tried to manoeuvre my way subtly into position near her. Unfortunately, as is their way, one of the Americans—who over the course of the week was to become a distinct pain in the arse—took it upon himself to march right up to her and start talking at her. Not to her, but *at* her, displaying consummate mastery of a technique they appear to have researched, invented, developed and patented ever since they realised that there existed a world outside of their own and that they had better start spreading the word about how it paled in comparison.

In order to get the chat flowing, it was decided to seat an Anglo beside a Spaniard on the coach for the journey westwards. We weren't of equal number however, some Spaniards having decided to make their own way to the hotel, so I was left on my sweeney todd for the duration of the trip. Unperturbed, I read my book[1] and took in the scenery. On arrival, we were assigned our rooms and given an hour to freshen up before gathering in the meting room for a plenary session, which was to be hosted by Richard Vaughan, the big cheese whose brainchild this whole operation was.[2] As he gave his spiel I surveyed my object of desire. Beautiful tanned skin. Dark eyes. Little button nose. Generously full, but not overly boisterous lips. Gentle features; great smile. She radiated warmth and sincerity. So entranced with her was I, that I didn't hear the main man call my name when it came to my turn to stand up and say a few words of introduction to my companions for the week. Snapping out of my reverie, I raised my hand and did the necessary, addressing my every word in one direction only.

1. *A Million Little Pieces* by James Frey. Totally devastating. A must read.

2. Quite a brainchild it was too—during the week I learned that the Spaniards, or more accurately, their employers, paid the not insignificant sum of €1800 to attend the course. There were 22 of them present the week I was there. And the week before, and the week before that. And there would be 22 more there the week after. And this was one of two locations he was running. As well as individual and group lessons during the week in eight different locations throughout Spain.

He finally wrapped things up by saying that it was customary for him to seat everybody at dinner the first night—'just a little thing I like to do'.

I sidled out of the room a few steps behind her and remained there as we made our way back to the main block of the hotel. We entered the dining room to find Dickie holding court, directing people to various tables, which I noted with some disappointment, were set for four or six and not two. Bloody group cohesion. How was I supposed to get a little one-on-one action going on? He directed her to a table by the far wall and then requested an Anglo to join her. Naturally, I volunteered my services, which necessitated shouldering a rather portly American to one side.

We were joined at our table by another Spaniard and another Anglo, both of whom I tried to ignore for as long as possible until I got the SP on the lovely lady sitting opposite me. Anxious as I was to get cracking on the biographical compilation, I was conscious that English was her second language, the nuances of which she was only in the process of acquiring. Keen not to make her feel inadequate or ill-equipped for the week ahead, I tried to kick off with a few easy Starters for Ten. I hadn't got very far (Name: Catalina. Place of residence: Navarra, northern Spain. Occupation: printer), when the other pair started muscling in, all gung-ho for a bit of cross-table chatter. Barely concealing my resentment at having to share my new toy, I threw in a few contributions as the starters arrived, and then went looking for a bottle of wine.

And now for an amazing coincidence of earth-shattering proportions, requiring nothing less than a bi-millennial aligning of Venus and Saturn: the printing company she worked for conducted most of its business outside of Spain—hence her need to improve her English—and one of their customers was none other than Gill & Macmillan in Dublin, publishers of this very tome! How whacked is that? Needless to say, I pounced on this information to modestly let her know of my association with her client company. At first she didn't understand me and thought she had miscommunicated something, but when she finally realised the significance of the coincidence, she was suitably gobsmacked, and beamed in my direction a smile of such warmth that I almost melted.

I battled hard to keep the conversation within the parameters of our newly discovered common ground, determined to mine its every seam for all that it was worth, mostly because I was genuinely interested in her job and the industry she worked in, but also because it excluded the other pair at our table, who were so inconsiderate and so bereft of tact that it didn't even dawn on them to sod off and sit somewhere else. But Catalina was the kind of gentle soul that embraced all manner of people, obviously flawed as they were, and chatted away somewhat falteringly to all present at the table. Meal over, we repaired to the lobby bar for tea and coffee. As I've said before, I drink neither, but as we sauntered upstairs I suggested to Catalina that she stake a claim on one of the sofas in the lobby whilst I got her a coffee. Impressed with my chivalrous qualities, she happily agreed and I went to get the beverages, discreetly but determinedly skipping the queue, anxious to return as quickly as possible before some other chancer decided to have a crack at her.

The lobby was an airy, spacious high-ceilinged affair and was generously appointed with a number of deep, comfy looking sofas arranged around large square coffee tables. I was pleased to note that Catalina had chosen a sofa far from the chattering rabble, and when I returned with the drinks I casually sat down beside her so we could resume our conversation in peace. Gregarious lot that they were, an assortment of characters rambled over in our direction from time to time. We entertained them well enough and when they left, resumed our easy-going and wide-ranging conversation, like neighbourhood friends reunited after a long spell apart.

We had an early start the following morning—every morning in fact—and after an hour or so Catalina, regretfully I thought, excused herself, saying she was tired and had to telephone her family. My thoughts exactly: what family? There had been no mention of a significant other thus far, and no wedding band graced her elegant fourth finger. I heeded my own good counsel, said nothing, and wished her a good night. Once she had departed I headed towards the bar and the large group of people still there, chatting away excitedly. Though exhausted myself, I thought it wise to put in a bit of spadework with the group at large, to suss out what the competition was like. Half an hour did it, and satisfied with my progress thus far, I too retired to my quarters.

Early-morning alarm calls are not my forte at all, it has to be said, and I arrived to breakfast the following morning a mere twenty minutes before it was finished and we were due to assemble in the lobby for our first tutorials proper. I spotted Catalina seated at a table of four. A little miffed that none of them would give up their seat to me, I settled for breakfasting with a pleasant pair of Spaniards at a table nearby. At ten o'clock we all gathered by a notice board in the lobby to see who we were assigned to speak with for the following hour. Scanning the list of names, I noted with glee that I was down to speak with Catalina from eleven to twelve: a whole hour! No interruptions, no forced group activity. Just me and her—a perfect opportunity to cement the undeniable bond that had already formed between us at this early stage.

'I have you next,' she said, smiling at me.

You had me last night, beautiful.

'Yeah, that's right. I can't wait. See you in an hour,' I said as I set off for a walk with my first pupil, an airline pilot with Iberia called Miguel.

Miguel's English was very good, as I later discovered was the case with the vast majority of the Spaniards enrolled on the programme. Their principal difficulties were accent differentiation and confidence in their own ability. Consummate communicator that I am, I put him at ease straight away and spoke concisely with perfect diction. I had had some reservations about how much I thought I would get out of the week, but I have to say that after that first hour, I was delighted I had signed up for it. As the week progressed, I got quite a kick out of each of my pupils telling me how easily they understood me. Fair enough, I wasn't speaking as fast as I usually did, and I wasn't using as many short cuts as I would when talking to my fellow countrymen, but neither was I dumbing it down to playschool level by any stretch.

I returned to the lobby to spot Catalina anxiously scanning the assembled group, obviously desperate not to miss one minute of our precious time together.

'Hi,' I said cheerily as I strolled up behind her, resisting the overwhelming desire I had to smell her hair and kiss her slender neck.

'Hello,' she said politely.

'Shall we take a walk?' I asked, in a manner reminiscent of a Victorian gentleman courting a society lady.

'Yes, that would be good,' she agreed, and we set off around the grounds of the hotel and out onto the small country road that led up towards the mountains.

During that hour, from eleven to twelve, on that beautiful crisp morning, to the sound of birds singing and fresh water gurgling in a nearby stream, I finally found what it was that I felt I had been looking for. I would have happily walked barefoot back to Madrid with Catalina, so captivated by her personality as I was. It turned out she was actually 36; 37 in a few weeks' time. (I didn't believe her until she showed me her driving licence, which I scanned intensely, committing her date of birth to memory.) And she was married. Happily so, it appeared, with two children. A girl aged 10, and a boy aged 8. I'd only known her a couple of hours, but I knew her husband was the luckiest man alive. She was a contented individual, sure of her place in the world and her immediate role in it. Hardworking, intelligent, outgoing, funny, warm, sincere, beautiful. Beautiful. Did I say she was beautiful? And not just in an aesthetic way: she was a beautiful person, all told. She was exactly what I wanted. And I know I said before I didn't want anything to do with kids, and that this is going to sound terribly Oprah-esque, but for the first time in my life I could see the positive effects of having children. Catalina was a better, more complete, more evolved woman because of her children. Their existence gave her an extra dimension. I suppose that's true for all women, but I'd never considered it before.

All too soon, our hour was up and we returned to the hotel. As Catalina started off on another walk with another Anglo, I scanned the notice board for my next appointment, watching her disappear slowly over the crest of the hill. She was a tough act to follow.

And so began a routine that was to last for the following six days. Breakfast from 9 to 10, followed by four hours of one-to-ones from 10 until 2. Lunch from 2 to 3.30, with siesta or free time until 5. Group activity from 5 to 6. More one-to-ones until 8.

Group entertainment from 8 to 9. Dinner from 9 to 10.30. After dinner you were free to go to bed if you wished, but as is the way with these types of things, this was quite often the best part of the day, when everybody, free from the shackles of scheduled activity, could relax and be themselves, talking freely with their newly made friends. Needless to say, all my after dinner time was spent on the sofa with Catalina and Elisa—another very cool Spaniard from Madrid Catalina had introduced me to—and a small group of people, mostly Spaniards, that we had become close to, sometimes to the annoyance and consternation of some of the other Anglos present, who seemed a little miffed at how tight a group we'd become. So much so that at one point during the week, the project leader called me aside and told me to stop spending so much time with Catalina. The following evening she told me that he had said the same thing to her. In reply, she had told him that she was there to learn English and that that was exactly what she was doing, inviting him to join us for a drink if he needed reassurance.

And she was right—all we did was talk. Much as the thoughts of being intimate with Catalina haunted my every night that week, I knew I had to accept that she was loved by another. (Another who had beaten me to her by 15 years as well, the lucky sod.) I tried to take solace in the fact that whatever about her availability—nil—I should have been ecstatic to have finally met someone who embodied all I wanted in a soulmate/lover/girlfriend/partner/confidante. But it was hard. It was like finally being in a position to buy my much coveted Jaeger-LeCoultre Reverso Duo, only to be told that the one in the window was the last one available, and that it had already been sold. Well, no, strike that, that's a crap analogy. It was just hard. Here she was, all I wanted in the whole world, and I couldn't have her. Maybe even if she was available she wouldn't want anything to do with me—it's happened before, but never deterred me from giving it a shot—but that didn't matter. What mattered was that I couldn't even attempt to make the leap I had stalled making before. Right when I was all set to jump and all, regardless of how far it was to the other side.

All too soon, Friday rolled around and the week in Barco de Avila was over. Shortly after noon, after the 'graduation' ceremony, I took David, one of the Spaniards, up on his offer of a lift back to Madrid, principally because it meant I could get out of there a couple of hours before the coach was due to bring us back, but also because Catalina and Elisa were going with him. Catalina's train was not leaving until 7 that evening. I was staying the night in Madrid before heading home the following day, so we decided to spend the day together hanging out before her train departed northwards. David dropped Elisa off and we said our goodbyes, but not before I arranged to meet her the following morning for a walking tour of her native city before my flight back to Dublin, and then he dropped Catalina and I off at a restaurant recommended to us by Elisa which apparently served a great Spanish omelette, a dish I had become partial to during the week.

As we enjoyed a long, lazy lunch we tried to figure out how to spend the day. Laden down with luggage we didn't want to haul around with us for the afternoon, I suggested renting a room in a hostel to dump our bags in before setting off. Catalina went one better though and rang a friend of hers who worked with a large hotel chain. Her friend made a few calls and okayed it for us to leave our cumbersome bags in a hotel ten minutes from Atocha train station. Unburdened, we strolled happily through the city for an hour or so and then decamped to the terrace of a nearby tapas bar, where we sat for four hours, chatting away whilst enjoying a few drinks. Free of the near tyrannical schedule of the English language programme, Catalina was much more relaxed and at ease, gliding effortlessly from topic to topic in her dramatically improved conversational English. She was even beginning to pepper some of her sentences with words like 'cool' and 'shit', just like a native English speaker: I beamed with pride at the positive impact I had on her during the week.

The hours ticked by all too quickly, and soon it was time to get a taxi to the train station. Passing our last few minutes together having one last drink in a café on the lower level, I was suddenly struck with a horrible thought: I may never see this woman again. Numbed by the horror of such a prospect, I averted my eyes from the direction they had been locked in all week—looking directly at

Catalina—and turned away: if she could read my mind I was in big trouble. The flaps on the departures board twirled around, informing me of her imminent departure. I took her case and we walked silently to the security check in area. Promising to stay in touch by phone and e-mail and to meet up somewhere, sometime, soon, we said our goodbyes with a hug and a kiss. She turned away slowly, joined the crowd milling through the gate, and eventually disappeared in the swarm of evening commuters.

I went outside, slumped to the ground and had a cigarette. And then another one. And then another.

———

I arrived back in Dublin considerably down-in-the-mouth, with the dreary late-January skies threatening to open up on me at any minute. A pile of mail, both of the snail and electronic variety, awaited me when I got home, but I couldn't be bothered dealing with it and went straight to bed.

I slouched around the house for the next week or so, feeling inordinately sorry for myself, balefully bemoaning the fact that after all the lengths I'd gone to in the previous year to meet someone, the one woman I met who I totally connected with was happily married.

As is the way with most people, once January was over and done with, hope sprang anew. Paul called around one of the evenings on his way home from work and we ordered some food. He'd been away at some incredibly boring conference in the States early in January and I'd headed off again before he got home, so we hadn't actually caught up since before I'd done a bunk for the festive season. We cracked open a beer and filled each other in on what had been going on. Rachel was pregnant again, he told me proudly, openly marveling at his virility. I was telling him about my tutoring in Spain when the doorbell rang.

'Grub's up,' I said, jumping up to get my wallet.

I opened the door and took the steaming bag from the Oriental delivery driver, who was hopping giddily from left to right, turning around to smile at the passengers in his car, who were all laughing and chattering away giddily.

'Hi, how's it going? How much is that?' I asked.

'Is €18.70 please,' he replied.

'There you go, that's grand,' I said, handing him €20.

'Thanks very much,' he said, turning to go back to his idling car. 'Happy New Year.'

'Sorry?'

'Happy New Year. Is Chinese New Year, yeah?'

'Oh, right. Cool, cheers. Happy New Year.'

Time to start whittling.